BLOCK 3   INTRODUCTION

> The unavoidable consequence of human social life is a realization of the essentially private and subjective nature of our experiences of the world coupled with a strong wish to break out of that privacy and establish contact with another mind. Personal relationships hold out to their members the possibility, though perhaps rarely realized in full, of establishing such contact.

(Kelley, 1979, p. 169)

Our relationships with others – whether with relatives, friends, colleagues, strangers, enemies or spouses – can provide us with some of our most rewarding and our most distressing experiences. We all recognize just what a fundamental part these relationships play in our social lives; very often severe psychological and physical distress can be caused by disruptions in our personal relationships. Lynch (1977) and Bloom *et al.* (1978), for example, have demonstrated that people whose relationships are in disorder or under tension often experience a greater amount of illness than people whose relationships are in good repair. It is clear that, from the perspectives of satisfaction and of health, personal relationships and their healthy development should be of major concern to psychologists.

Poets and novelists have reflected for many centuries on the meaning of love, friendship and other personal relationships, on their qualities, and how they are developed and maintained. Psychologists, on the other hand, have only turned their attention to these questions relatively recently. Many people feel that such efforts by psychologists are bound to be wasted. They feel that most of what there is to be known about personal relationships is already common knowledge, and that the psychological study of these questions will not lead us any further. However, it remains the case that, although we have many insights from writers like Shakespeare, Tolstoy or Jane Austen, our knowledge about personal relationships has advanced very little beyond what they were able to tell us. Literature has not provided any *systematic* guidance about the best ways of conducting relationships, or of preventing the disasters in relationships which can lead to serious consequences such as suicide. Whilst literature has provided many insights about the personal experience of the joys and problems of relationships, it is the job of systematic psychological research to try to test out these insights and to pull them together in order to establish meaningful theories of relationship development and decline. For instance, common sense tells us that 'Birds of a feather flock together' *and* that 'Opposites attract'. Surely it is worth while exploring such contradictions to establish which is most valid. It is only through a detailed and systematic study of personal relationships that psychologists can hope to make a practical contribution towards understanding such problems as the increase in the divorce rate, and provide information to help counsellors advising people whose relationships continually go wrong.

This Block describes research that has been done by psychologists in the area of relationships. You should try to assess how successful you think they have been in attempting to produce valid and generalizable accounts of the way in which relationships develop. Try to keep in mind the following three dimensions with which to assess each theory or school of research:

(a) *Aims* What were the theories (or types of research) trying to achieve? Some theories aim to account for the whole process of relationship development, others only account for specific events or processes in relationships. The latters' aims are bound to be more limited, but the success of a theory has to be considered in relation to its aims.

(b) *Methods* How adequately do you feel the theories are tested? Are the methods which the researchers use the best methods available? What might be the ethical problems with the methods used, or the alternative methods? What subjects do the researchers use? You will find that most of the work has been done with students, and you should try to assess whether or not their results can then be generalized to other populations, such as old people, other cultures, or the handicapped community.

(c) *Relevance to real life* Try to assess how useful the findings of the research might be in real life. Earlier the point was made that literature and common sense have provided many insights into personal relationships, but psychology aims to provide a systematic account that will be of *more use* in helping people with relationship problems. Do you think that current research reported here actually meets these aims? If not, where are the weak points? You may feel that these 'gaps' in our understanding will be filled once newly developed methods become more established and are applied to wider populations, or you may feel that the research is actually heading the wrong way. Try and think about what research in this area *ought* to be doing to be relevant to real life.

The Block is structured into two main parts. Units 8 and 9 examine two major theories, personal construct theory and attribution theory, which are fully worked out models of how we try to understand our social world, and in particular, how we explain to ourselves the causes of other people's actions. The theories are discussed separately, but at several points you are encouraged to compare and contrast them.

The second part of the Block – Unit 10/11 – examines the scope of research which is more wide-ranging and describes various research that has been undertaken on the nature of personal relationships. Three models of social behaviour are discussed initially: the economic model, the dramaturgical model and information-gathering approaches; representative research in each tradition is presented. Work on more naturalistic relationships and disorders in relationships is then presented.

More detailed introductions and study guides than can be given here precede each Unit, with specific objectives at the outset, and sections returning to these objectives at the end.

References

BLOOM, B., ASHER, S. and WHITE, S. (1978) 'Marital disruption as a stressor: a review and analysis', *Psychological Bulletin*, Vol. 85, pp. 867–94.

KELLEY, H. H. (1979) *Personal Relationships: Their Structures and Processes*, New York, Halsted Press.

LYNCH, J. J. (1977) *The Broken Heart: The Medical Consequences of Loneliness*, New York, Basic Books.

BLOCK 3 UNDERSTANDING OTHER PEOPLE AND DEVELOPING RELATIONSHIPS

BLOCK INTRODUCTION

UNIT 8 UNDERSTANDING OTHERS I: A PERSONAL CONSTRUCT THEORY ACCOUNT

Prepared for the course team by Barbara Thompson

UNIT 9 UNDERSTANDING OTHERS II: THE APPROACH OF ATTRIBUTION THEORY

Prepared for the course team by Charles Antaki

SOCIAL SCIENCES: A THIRD LEVEL COURSE
SOCIAL PSYCHOLOGY: DEVELOPMENT, EXPERIENCE
AND BEHAVIOUR IN A SOCIAL WORLD

THE OPEN UNIVERSITY PRESS

Open University Course Team

Melanie Bayley   *Editor*
Hedy Brown   *Senior lecturer in social psychology*
Rudi Dallos   *Staff tutor, Region 03*
David Graddol   *Research Fellow, School of Education*
Judith Greene   *Professor of psychology*
Jane Henry   *Lecturer in educational technology*
Pam Higgins   *Designer*
Clive Holloway   *BBC producer*
Tom Hunter   *Editor*
Mary John   *Staff tutor, Region 02*
Maggie Lawson   *Project control*
Dorothy Miell   *Lecturer in psychology*
Eleanor Morris   *BBC producer*
Stella Pilsworth   *Liaison librarian*
Ortenz Rose   *Secretary*
Roger J. Sapsford   *Lecturer in research methods*
David Seligman   *BBC executive producer*
Ingrid Slack   *Course manager*
Richard Stevens   *Senior lecturer in psychology*

Kerry Thomas   *Lecturer in psychology, Course team chairperson*
Barbara Thompson   *Staff tutor, Region 01*
Eleanor Thompson   *Project control*
Pat Vasiliou   *Secretary*
Doreen Warwick   *Secretary*
Chris Wooldridge   *Editor*

External Course Team Member
Jeannette Murphy   *Polytechnic of North London*

Consultants
Charles Antaki   *University of Lancaster*
Glynis M. Breakwell   *University of Surrey*
Steve Duck   *University of Lancaster*
Susan Gregory   *University of Nottingham*
Patrick Humphreys   *London School of Economics*
Kim Plunkett   *University of Aarhus, Denmark*
Harry Procter   *Southwood Hospital, Bridgewater*

Course Assessor
Professor Robert Farr   *London School of Economics*

Set reading
Unit 9
M. Lalljee (1981) 'Attribution theory and the analysis of explanations', in Antaki, C. (ed.) (1981) *The Psychology of Ordinary Explanations*, New York and London, Academic Press, Ch. 5, pp. 119–38.

The Open University
Walton Hall, Milton Keynes
MK7 6AA

First published 1984. Reprinted 1988, 1991

Copyright © 1984   The Open University

Designed by the Graphic Design Group of the Open University.

Printed in Great Britain by Staples Printers St Albans Limited at The Priory Press.

ISBN 0 335 12223 X

This text forms part of an Open University course. The complete list of Blocks and Units in the course appears on the back cover.

For general availability of supporting material referred to in this text, please write to Open University Educational Enterprises Limited, 12 Cofferidge Close, Stony Stratford, Milton Keynes, MK11 1BY, Great Britain.

Further information on Open University courses may be obtained from the Admissions Office, The Open University, P.O. Box 48, Walton Hall, Milton Keynes MK7 6AB.

1.3

UNIT 8
UNDERSTANDING OTHERS I:
A PERSONAL CONSTRUCT
THEORY ACCOUNT

*Prepared for the course team
by Barbara Thompson*

CONTENTS

Objectives

After studying this Unit you should be able to:

1 Describe the main principles of personal construct theory.

2 Understand the philosophy underlying the theory and the methodology associated with it.

3 Understand how the construct system of the individual influences the way s/he perceives and relates to others.

4 Recognize that this is a dynamic and interactive process.

5 Evaluate the contribution of personal construct theory in explaining how people understand others.

6 Explore your own construct system and try to understand how it is similar to or different from others'.

Study guide

Personal construct theory, like attribution theories which you will be studying in the next Unit, is concerned with how we come to understand others. Whilst personal construct theory tries to get inside the heads of individuals and to understand the way each of us experiences the world, and especially our fellow beings, attribution theories stand 'outside' the person: they use this 'outside perspective' to examine the strategies which people in general use when trying to make sense of others. As you will see when you read Unit 9, attribution theories are rooted in experimental social psychology, and use laboratory-based techniques to obtain 'objective' data: their aim is to seek general rules about the processes of attribution. Personal construct theory, on the other hand, originated in clinical psychology, and the techniques it uses are based on the need to explore individuals' constructions of the world.

As you study this Unit and the next, you will need to bear in mind that the philosophy which underlies personal construct theory is very different from that on which attribution theories are based. This difference may well be the reason for the different styles adopted by the people who write about them. By the time you reach the end of Unit 9 you should have some idea of the advantages and disadvantages of each approach, and have given some thought to the question as to whether the theories are complementary or contradictory.

If you find that you are interested in the approach of personal construct theory, you will have a chance of learning more about it by doing the Kelly Project option.

1 AN INTRODUCTION TO PERSONAL CONSTRUCT THEORY

How do we come to understand others? One view is that people have enduring personality characteristics – introvert or extrovert, generous or mean – and that once we have correctly labelled someone's characteristics we will then have all the essential information about that person. Another view associated with, amongst others, George Kelly (1955) is that people are constantly developing and changing, and that to understand someone we have to try to find out how that person makes sense of the world.

Underlying these views there are very different assumptions about the nature of people. The first view can crudely be categorized as the 'person as object', possessing certain characteristics, whose behaviour results from pressures from biological or social forces. On the other hand, Kelly's view of people is that they are active initiators of action. He was concerned by the way some psychologists seemed to have two different models of people, one which they used to explain the people they were studying (which was similar to the 'person as object' view described above), and one of the 'person as scientist', which they used to explain their own behaviour when being 'psychologists'. Faced with this apparent discrepancy, Kelly asked what would happen if one started from the assumption that *everyone* is like the scientist, actively exploring the world to try to understand what is going on. This was the starting point for the development of personal construct theory.

Attribution theories (which will be discussed in the next Unit) also treat ordinary people as 'naive' scientists, but they use a rather different model of science from the one used in personal construct theory. Whereas attribution theories start from the assumption that there are general rules determining the correct (or optimal) strategies that all people should use when making inferences, the 'scientist' in personal construct theory is trying to test out the usefulness of her/his own unique current model of reality.

According to personal construct theory, 'Although there is a real world external to our perceptions of it, the way we . . . come to know the world is by placing our own interpretations upon it' (Epting, 1984, p. 24). On the basis of these we construct **model of the world** models of the world (sometimes referred to as internal representations of the world) which can then be used to anticipate what is likely to happen and thus guide our behaviour. Notice that we are no longer speaking only of perceiving *people*, the same process is involved whatever you are looking at: you interpret the images which impinge on your retina on the basis of your previous experience, in other words you make *hypotheses* about what it is you think you are seeing. To take an exaggerated example, think of those pictures of objects in extreme close-up which are often the subject of questions in television quiz games. As you try to identify them you test the impressions you perceive against the various models you have stored. Sometimes, inevitably, you are mistaken. Look at the picture in Figure 1. People normally perceive it to be a chair, and yet in fact it is only a collection of disjointed rods and wires. If we can make such errors with simple objects like chairs, how much greater is the problem we face in trying to **constructive** understand people? It is evidence of this kind which led Kelly to postulate con-**alternativism** structive alternativism (which is what he called the philosophical basis of personal construct theory): that is, we are capable of construing our experiences in as great a variety of ways 'as our wits will enable us to contrive' (Kelly, 1970, p. 1).

Because Kelly's early academic training was in mathematics and physics, he **fundamental postulate** chose to set out his theory in a very formal way with a fundamental postulate – a statement which puts forward the basic principle of the theory – and a number of **corollary** corollaries, which follow from and elaborate this principle. I shall not be discuss-

Figure 1 The Ames chair demonstration. Above: from behind the apparatus. Below: from the viewing point.

Source: Ittelson, 1968

ing all aspects of the theory here, but rather will focus on those which help explain how we understand other people and hence relate to them.

The fundamental postulate of personal construct theory is:

> *A person's processes are psychologically channelized by the ways in which s/he anticipates events.*

This means that everything people think, feel or do (their 'processes') results from their attempts to understand what is going on. As the word 'channelized' implies, these processes operate through a network of pathways which are a consequence of their predictions about what will occur. This is the metaphor of the 'person as scientist' referred to earlier. Kelly justifies using this metaphor by comparing the activities of ordinary people (that is, lay scientists or 'ordinary explainers') to those of people who are acknowledged scientists:

> ... both seek to anticipate events. Both have their theories, in terms of which they attempt to structure the current occurrences. Both hypothesize. Both observe. Both reluctantly revise their predictions in the light of what they observe, on the one hand, and the extent of their theoretical investment on the other.

(Kelly, 1980, p. 24)

People usually approach someone new with a set of expectations based on what has happened in previous relationships. Some of these are of the very general kind, such as 'Most people are nice if you treat them right'; others are more specific, perhaps based on previously available information about the person: 'If he's a friend of Joe's, he's probably a bore'; 'She's supposed to be a real high-flyer'. As we interact with the person concerned, we observe their behaviour and revise our model in the light of what we see. The particular things we look for will depend on what we have found to be good predictors in the past. My father, for example, set great store by a person's handshake: if it was limp, they were almost immediately categorized as weak and indecisive.

Scientists studying the way we perceive people use similar methods to these, as you will see throughout the Block. They make hypotheses about what things people look for in a new acquaintance, what particular characteristics increase the probability that people will try to develop the relationship, and which, if any, rule out people as potential friends. In theory (although not always in practice) professional scientists search for evidence which *refutes* their theories; ordinary people, on the other hand, are more likely to look only for *confirmation*, with the risk that their hypotheses will be self-fulfilling. In addition, whereas professional scientists have traditionally been concerned with building up a body of knowledge which can be widely applied, ordinary people are primarily concerned with developing an adequate model for their own use in coping with the world.

construction corollary

According to Kelly these models are constructed by means of recognizing similarities and differences in their experiences. In the words of the first of his corollaries, the 'construction corollary':

A person anticipates events by construing their replications.

So from birth a child begins to build up her/his model by recognizing similarities and differences. Mary Tyler (1981) writes:

The youngest child gives audible evidence that he is aware when he is hungry and when he is not. If a recording of the sounds in the womb is played to crying new-born babies they are quietened, responding to the familiar in a strange world. (p. 33)

In this way the child begins to construe the world in terms of a number of (as yet unlabelled) dimensions which allow her/him to distinguish between experiences, and so decide how to act. These dimensions, which Kelly calls constructs, are

bipolar constructs

bipolar, that is they have two contrasting poles. In the extract above two such constructs are implied:

'hungry—not hungry'
'familiar—strange'

dichotomy corollary

The next corollary states:

A person's construction system is composed of a finite number of dichotomous constructs.

The 'construction system' refers to the collection of interlinked constructs which make up a person's model of the world. This corollary is one which has caused a great deal of misunderstanding. People tend to think that speaking in terms of *dichotomous constructs* implies that the world is really partitioned into things which are, for example, *either* good *or* bad, black *or* white etc. But in speaking of constructs, Kelly is not speaking of actual objects, events or people but of *the ways in which people make sense of those events.* A construct, he says, is:

> ... a reference axis devised by man for establishing a personal orientation toward the various events he encounters. It is not itself a category of events or even a focus of a class... Man can, in turn, use this portable device for ordering symbols along scales, for placing events into categories, or for defining classses in the various familiar ways that suit his needs ... the construct is much more clearly a *psychological* guidance against which objects may be referred, than it is either a limited collection of things or a common essence distilled out of them.

(Kelly, 1979, p. 11; emphasis added)

The abstract nature of constructs is a rather slippery notion. This is partly due to the structure of our language. Thus, if I say, 'John is friendly', it is tempting to draw the conclusion that the 'friendliness' is a characteristic which is part of John rather than a construct which *I* am using to interpret his behaviour. Some doubt is thrown on the idea that friendliness is a characteristic of John when a colleague says, 'Do you think so? I find him most stand-offish.' Am I right? Is my colleague right? Actually, friendliness and stand-offishness are better construed as the ways in which each of us tries to make sense of John's behaviour towards us; these will reflect our different expectations of and behaviour towards him, as well as the way he construes us. Suppose John is a new senior member of staff. My experiences, which are, of course, affected by my age and status, have led me to assume that most people are really quite friendly, so I expect John to be. I walk up to him smiling and introduce myself and he responds. My colleague is young and rather in awe of people of high status, so he hovers in the background. Not surprisingly he is not noticed and this leads him to construe John as stand-offish. Each of us, as a result of past experience, has made predictions about what a person such as John will be like, and these have guided the way in which we have behaved towards him. We have geared our behaviour in such a way as to make it highly probable that our predictions will be confirmed. If my younger colleague had decided to test his prediction about John by trying to *dis*prove it, perhaps by acting in a positive and friendly way towards him, the outcome might have been different.

In the above example I have used the construct 'friendly—stand-offish' and indicated to you that this is one of the dimensions that I use in making sense of the world. Notice that by bringing in my hypothetical colleague (could he be me some years ago?), I have ensured that you have both poles of the construct. This should be of more help to you in understanding how I am using the construct than if I had used only one pole, say friendly. Although you would have clearly had some idea what I meant, you might have assumed that I meant friendly as opposed to shy or hostile. A construct derives its meaning from *both poles.* Kelly differentiates constructs from concepts. A concept, for instance book, can be seen as dividing the world into two parts, one which contains all those things which are examples of the concept, all the books, and the other which contains everything else. A construct on the other hand assumes that similarities can only be understood in the context of differences. So the construct 'black-skinned—white-skinned' will have no meaning for me if I have only ever experienced people with black skins. It is said that when the Australian Aborigines first saw white-skinned people they did not construe them as people but as spirits. The idea that there could be people with white skin came much later, and with it, one assumes, the construct 'black-skinned—white-skinned'.

A construct, therefore, partitions the world three ways, dividing it into those things which are like the left side of the construct or *similarity pole* (in the example, friendly) and those which are like the right side or *contrast pole* (stand-offish), *and* those to which the construct does not apply, or, to use Kelly's phrase, **range of convenience**   are 'outside its range of convenience'. So I may be able to apply my construct

focus of convenience friendly—stand-offish to people and animals, but not to books, flowers or furniture. Of course, the slightly different construct of 'friendly—hostile' might have a different range of convenience. I can speak about a landscape being friendly or hostile, but, to me at least, a landscape is not stand-offish. A related term, focus of convenience, is used to refer to those elements to which the construct is maximally useful and appropriate, often those which originally led to the construct being formed.

element The commonest way to find out which constructs a person uses to make sense of a particular aspect of the world, for example other people, is to ask them to name three people that they know well and to tell you some important way in which two of them are similar to one another and yet different from the third. The method is derived from Kelly's view that constructs can only come into being in the context of a minimum of three events or 'elements', two of which are alike and one different. The elements can be people, objects, situations or events, depending on which aspect of the world you are interested in construing.

ACTIVITY 2   (15–25 minutes)

Stop for a moment and explore some of the ways in which you construe people. Take three slips of paper and on each of them write the name of a person you know well. Don't make the task too difficult for yourself at this stage by choosing people you think of as similar to each other. One possibility might be 'yourself', a 'friend' and 'someone you know well . . . but whom you do not consider to be a friend'. For example, suppose I chose myself, Rosemary and my boss. When asked to think of some important way in which I think two of them are like one another but different from the third, I might say that Rosemary and I are alike because we tend to be disorganized; my boss is different because he is very well-organized. My boss and I are alike, however, because we are both hopeless at practical things whereas Rosemary is very handy. So I can begin to produce a list of how I construe these people that looks like this:

	Myself	*Rosemary*	*My boss*	
tend to be disorganized	✓	✓	×	very well-organized
hopeless at practical things	✓	×	✓	very handy

The ticks show the two people who are alike, and the way they are alike is written on the left, which you will remember is the *similarity* pole of the construct. The cross indicates the person who is different and the way in which s/he differs is written on the right, the *contrast* pole.

Now try this for yourself. Start by thinking of a way of importance to you in which two of the people you have chosen are alike and different from the third. Put ticks under the names of the two people who are alike and a cross under the other. Write the way the two are alike in the similarity column and the way the third is different in the contrast column. Next time try to think of a way in which the person who was different on construct 1 is like one of the others, as I did in the example. Continue until you run out of ideas, time or patience.

	Names			
	1	2	3	
Similarities	....	....	....	*Contrasts*

1

2

3

4

5

6

triad You now have a list of some of the ways in which you think about people. Look at it carefully. Although it is derived on the basis of construing a very limited sample – just three people – it almost certainly contains a number of dimensions which you use in construing people in general. At the same time a number of other constructs will inevitably be missing. Do you think someone else construing these three people would have been likely to have thought of the same things? What about the actual words you used? If you did use the three people (the 'triad') I suggested (that is, a friend, yourself and someone you do not know so well), did you find it easier to think of ways in which you and your friend were similar to each other and different from the person who is not a friend, than ways in which the latter was like either of you?

---

organization corollary Of course, we don't just have constructs lying around in random piles. Rather, our constructs tend to be related to each other in systematic ways. The 'organization corollary' says:

> *Each person characteristically evolves for her/his convenience in anticipating events, a construction system embracing ordinal relationships between constructs.*

In discussing this corollary, I would like first to focus on the idea of relationships between constructs and after that consider the fact that some relationships are 'ordinal' (in this case, this means hierarchical).

In abstracting similarities and differences from our experience we soon discover that certain dimensions frequently appear in association with one another. So people may assume that someone who is physically attractive is also interesting to be with, and/or that they lead an exciting life. Or, as I myself do, they may expect people who are physically attractive to be arrogant and insensitive, having had things their own way for too long. So, when I construe someone as physically attractive, I also expect to construe them as arrogant and insensitive. The fact that constructs are related in an orderly manner helps us to elucidate further what a person means by a particular construct. So if I know that for a particular teacher the construct 'extrovert—introvert' and 'active in class—takes little part' are closely related, when she tells me a pupil is extroverted, I will also know that she finds him a good person to have in her class (incidently a very different point of view from that taken by most teachers in a study I carried out). At the same time knowing how constructs are related may help us understand why a person persists in a particular kind of behaviour. For example, suppose Pete is constantly criticized for being unreliable. If we were to investigate his construct system, we might find that the construct 'unreliable—reliable' was strongly related to the constructs 'spontaneous—predictable' and 'interesting—boring'. Although he may want to become more reliable, he may find it difficult because such a change implicitly carries with it the danger that he will become boringly predictable.

ordinal relationship between constructs There is, however, more to the claim that constructs are organized than the fact that certain constructs are used in association with one another. The organization corollary quoted above states that there are ordinal (or hierarchical) relationships between constructs. This implies that certain constructs *play a more important role* in our understanding of the world than others. One way of finding out which are the more important constructs is to use a technique called **laddering** *laddering* developed by Hinkle (1965). In this technique when a person has elicited a number of her constructs about people she is then asked on which pole of the construct she would prefer to see herself. For example, if the original construct is 'friendly—stand-offish', and the person has said she would prefer to be seen as friendly, she is then asked why and a further construct is elicited. The reason may be that friendly people are easy to get to know, whereas stand-offish people are hard to get to know. Again the person is asked to indicate the preferred pole of this construct ('easy to get to know—hard to get to know') and to give a reason for her preference, and so on, until she can go no further. For example, take the first construct in my example in Activity 2, 'tends to be disorganized—very well-organized'. If asked which I would prefer to be, I might say I preferred to be a bit disorganized because to me being very well-organized is associated with inflexibility, whereas some degree of disorganization indicates flexibility: the next construct in my hierarchy would thus be 'flexible—inflexible'. Asked for a preference here, I might say that I would prefer to be flexible, because flexible people are accepting and tolerant, whereas inflexible people are rejecting and intolerant.

ACTIVITY 3   (10 minutes)

Try this with some of the constructs you elicited in Activity 2. Select one of your constructs and ask yourself on which side of it you prefer to be. Then decide *why* you prefer this, eliciting a higher-order construct in the process. Repeat the process with this new construct and so on until you can go no further.

The higher up the hierarchy a construct is the more central it is said to be for that person's functioning. So judging by the example above, for me it is more important to be flexible than disorganized, and more important still to be accept-**core constructs** ing and tolerant. Constructs which are central are referred as 'core constructs'. Speaking of them Landfield and Leitner write:

> These are the most superordinate of our values and very much define our relationships with others. A person will act in relation to his core structures as if his life depended on it. (1980a, p. 8)

For this reason if one of a person's core constructs looks as if it is about to be invalidated s/he would become very alarmed. Indeed, Kelly defines threat as 'awareness of imminent comprehensive change in one's core structure'. So if one of the key characteristics of the person I see myself to be is tolerance, and someone accuses me of intolerance, I will feel as if my whole identity is under attack and try desperately to defend myself.

Thus far I have been concentrating on the structural aspects of the theory – what constructs are and how they relate to each other. But personal construct theory is, above all, a theory about *individual people*. At the end of Activity 2 I asked you whether you thought another person construing the same three people would be likely to have produced the same constructs as you did. In fact, unless you use constructs referring to very concrete characteristics, such as sex, hair colour or job, it is extremely unlikely that two people would produce the same or even similar constructs.

ACTIVITY 4   (15–25 minutes)

If you can find someone who is willing to do this with you, try eliciting five constructs each, about three people you both know well. Beware of using people who are very important to either of you unless you are prepared to be very, and perhaps painfully, honest with each other.

How similar are the two types of constructs? Do you think perhaps some of the constructs mean the same thing though they are expressed in rather different words? Is it possible that people are using the same words yet mean different things? Discuss the meanings and see how close you can come to finding out.

Kelly was always concerned to stress the *differences* between people. He claimed that even the so-called psychology of individual differences was more concerned with similarities between people, that is, it assumed that they could all be measured in terms of the same dimensions, like IQ or introversion-extroversion. The 'individuality corollary' states that:

individuality corollary

> *Persons differ from each other in their construction of events.*

Given that the theory assumes that each person develops their own model as a means of understanding the world, it woud be rather surprising if any two people were to do it in exactly the same way. Even people who appear to undergo similar experiences may select different information from them, and hence make different predictions for the future. Thus although, as suggested earlier, *all* babies will soon distinguish between being hungry and not being hungry, the *implications* that these two states come to have for them may be very different: for one baby being hungry may indicate that mother will soon come, while for another it may mean a long period of discomfort. How much more different will the construct systems of two adults be? After all, initial constructs form the basis of all later construing.

construing the world

Let us take our two babies as examples. The first baby feels hungry, he cries, mother comes and feeds him and generally makes him comfortable. He may well come to construe the world as a reliable sort of place and pretty well under his control. So when he gets older he may be much more willing to try new things and an important construct might be 'novel, exciting—ordinary, unexciting'. The second baby feels hungry and cries, but nothing happens; perhaps she is on a strict schedule. She may construe the world as a fairly hostile place totally outside her control, and one of her key constructs might be 'familiar, safe—strange, frightening'.

experience corollary

The 'experience corollary' states that:

> *A person's construction system varies as s/he successively construes the replication of events.*

My initial impression of a new acquaintance is that he is friendly and has had many interesting experiences. I meet him again and go to join him in the bar, whereupon he bombards me with detail after detail about the secondhand car he has just bought. I come away from the encounter with a somewhat changed view – still that he is friendly, but oh dear what a bore! Subsequent encounters may modify my construction of him further – if I risk engaging in them. In addition the relationship between the constructs 'has had interesting experiences' and 'is interesting to talk to' has been loosened a bit.

There is evidence that the type of constructs one uses about people changes as one gets to know them better. Whereas initially we use constructs to do with behaviour and physical appearance, later on in a relationship we are more likely to use ones concerned with more 'psychological' characteristics: see Box 1.

Box 1 Change in type of constructs as acquaintance progresses

In a series of studies of the constructs used at different points in the acquaintance process, Duck (1973) has shown that people use significantly fewer *psychological* constructs to describe people whom they have only just met than to describe people whom they have known over a longer period. Even fewer psychological constructs are used to describe well-known personalities whom they have never met: see Table 1. (See also Unit 9, section 3.) Instead they use *role* constructs, such as 'teachers—personnel managers', 'religious people—non-religious people', or constructs which refer to the ways they *interact* with others, such as 'good to talk to—boring'.

TABLE 1   Percentages of constructs assigned to four categories

Kinds of people being construed	Construct types			
	Psychological	*Role*	*Interaction*	*Other*
Distant public figures	38.06	50.00	5.32	6.41
New acquaintances who have just participated in a discussion	54.84	28.23	12.42	4.52
Well-known others*	63.04	24.42	6.24	6.40

Notes: *Data from a different, though comparable group of subjects.
(The statistical comparisons were made on the basis of the raw data, and not the percentages shown in this table.)

Source: Duck, 1973, p. 106, Table 9.1

The same sort of change seems to occur with age in children. Duck (1975) reported that the number of factual and physical constructs that children used decreased with age, and the number of psychological constructs they used increased. Similar findings are reported by Little (1968) who found that at about eleven years of age children used primarily 'physicalistic' constructs to describe people whereas in mid-adolescence psychological constructs prevail.

modulation corollary

A question which has to be asked, however, is, if we can only perceive the world through our construct systems, how can we ever escape the restrictions they place upon us and learn to see novel events? The 'modulation corollary' deals with this problem:

> *The variation in a person's construction system is limited by the permeability of the constructs within whose range of convenience the variants lie.*

permeability

'A permeable construct is one which is open to the inclusion of new events' (Bannister and Mair, 1968, p. 21) and variants are 'the old and new ways of construing' (ibid., p. 21). Thus a child has a superordinate construct of 'good—naughty'. When she is very young she construes people's statements as good if they are true, and naughty if they are lies. So when she is told the story used by Piaget (1932) of the child who reports having seen a dog as big as a cow, she construes it as naughty because it is untrue. As she grows older she begins to understand that there is another way in which to sort people's statements, that is according to whether they are *intended* to mislead or whether they are merely intended to entertain or give emphasis. According to the modulation corollary this new construction would not be possible if the superordinate construct 'good—naughty' was not permeable enough to accept the variant of construing in terms of intention within its range of convenience.

Remember that it is the way in which each construct is used which determines whether or not it is permeable, not the words used to label it. In her study of foreign women's adjustment to living in Hong Kong, Mildred McCoy (1980, 1981) found that at a particular stage of the adjustment process the women used the construct 'Chinese—own nationality' in a very impermeable way, with the label 'Chinese' necessarily implying a whole variety of negative characteristics. This made it most unlikely that any good could be perceived in someone who was Chinese. For some people this led to them leaving the country or trying to minimize contact with the indigenous people. Others fortunately managed gradually to modify their construction of the Chinese and their attitudes towards them, while not denying the existence of cultural differences. That is to say, after a period when their construct system is perceived as inadequate to cope with the new culture, and therefore under threat, it gradually becomes possible to modulate it sufficiently so that it can cope with the range of new events which the new culture has to offer.

At this stage of the discussion, we therefore seem to have a whole host of people each acting in the light of their own individual models of the world. But, if this is so, how can we ever understand each other sufficiently well to enable us to communicate with one another and to function as the social beings we unarguably are?

commonality corollary
The first point to make here is that although we do all differ from each other to some extent, there is usually much that is common. Kelly's 'commonality corollary' states:

> To the extent that one person employs a construction of experience which is similar to that employed by another, her/his processes are psychologically similar to those of the other person.

This means that the possibility exists that people will, under some circumstances, construe things similarly (remember the shared 'family constructs' in Unit 2, section 5.1). Indeed in many areas of life there is strong pressure to do so. One of the things parents do in bringing up children is to help them in their construction of experience. So a child learns to construe things as red or green, as hot or cold, good or naughty, safe or dangerous and so on. Many constructions depend on the society in which the person lives: to the English child grubs are probably construed as dirty, and not to be put in mouths; to some Australian Aboriginal children, however, certain grubs are very good food.

The fact that such similarities do exist provides a shared framework within which to *start* interacting and further negotiating the finer details of shared worlds. A number of studies starting within a Piagetian framework (Cooney and Selman, 1978; Clark and Delia, 1976) suggest that young children assume initially that everyone sees things the same way as they do, but that as they grow older they develop the ability to acknowledge the perspectives of other people.

consensual validation
personality support
Once we acknowledge that other people do construe things somewhat differently from the way we do, it becomes important to find out about these differences if we are to communicate effectively. This appears to be just what we are doing when we are getting to know someone. We try to find out what they are interested in, what their views are on things like politics and religion, what books they read, what work they do. And as well as being interested in the content of their answers, we listen to the ways in which they give them, trying to work out the construct systems which underlie them. There is a considerable amount of evidence (Duck, 1973) that we like people who construe things in much the same ways as we do. This is probably because the fact that they do so helps us to validate our model of the world. As our construction of the world to a large extent constitutes our identity, this also receives support. (Consensual validation and personality support are discussed in Unit 10/11, section 4.1.) Note that when we talk about 'similarity of construing' in this context we are talking about the extent to which people use the same constructs. So I may be happier discussing

my leisure reading with someone who, like me, construes books as 'easy to read—need effort', than someone who construes them as 'rubbish—worthwhile'. In other contexts, however, similarity of constructs may not be sufficient. For example, do you think my view of reality would be validated if, although you and I both agreed that the construct 'trustworthy—untrustworthy' was important in construing people, I construed a particular person as untrustworthy and you thought he was trustworthy?

In considering the commonality corollary it is very important to remember that it is not *experiencing* the same events which makes two people similar, it is *construing* the experience in the same way. A number of soldiers may all be engaged in the same action, but some may construe it as 'exciting' as opposed to 'boring', and others as 'terrifying' versus 'reassuring'. Only to the extent that they construe the experience similarly can their processes (their thoughts, feelings and actions) be said to be *psychologically* similar.

But how do we get to know whether or not someone is psychologically similar to us? This can only be done indirectly, that is, I can only construe you by means of my construct system, and in an attempt to understand you I will be testing hypotheses which I have generally found helpful in deciding what other people are like and whether they are likely to be the sort of people I can relate to. Initially the information I have to work on will be fairly superficial in character – for example, the way you look and behave – but this will not take me very far. Sooner or later it will be necessary to focus on psychological characteristics, and this will involve trying to construe your construct system. Since this is a very difficult undertaking, there may often be a temptation to assume that I understand what you mean, when really I have just translated what you are saying into my own constructs.

sociality corollary

At this point we have, of course, gone beyond the idea of simple overlap of construct systems or commonality, and it brings us to the corollary of personal construct theory which is central to its use in social psychology. This is the 'sociality corollary' which says:

> To the extent that one person construes the construction processes of another s/he may play a role in a social process involving the other person.

Role here is used in a different sense from that usually found in the sociological and psychological literature where it is defined as 'the pattern of behaviour expected by others from a person occupying a particular status' (Weeks, 1972, p. 57) or a set 'of norms, and norms are prescriptions for behaviour' (Brown, 1965, p. 154). It is somewhat closer to the concept of 'role-taking' originated by G. H. Mead, which is the process by which each individual is able to imaginatively cast her/himself in the roles of others and thereby anticipate their actions. But for Kelly it is not so much the roles of others you are casting yourself into by saying, 'What would I be doing in her place?', but rather, 'What would I be doing if I saw the world the way I think she does?'. Kelly says it is '. . . an on-going pattern of behaviour that follows from a person's understanding of how others who are associated with him in his tasks think' (Kelly, 1955, pp. 97–8).

Kelly is not saying that it is necessary for you to have a *correct* understanding of another person's behaviour in order to play a role in a social process with that person, although he is implying that the better the understanding, the more successful the interaction will be. If you simply assume, as it seems young children do, that everyone thinks the same way as you do yourself, there will be times when it works all right but others when there will almost certainly be misunderstandings. If only one of the partners in an interaction is able to construe the other's construction of events, s/he may be in a good position to manipulate the other if s/he is so minded. This would often be the case with a successful confidence trickster. You may, of course, have an excellent understanding of someone's construct system with respect to some aspect of life and know little about others. Members of a highly skilled football team seem to have an uncanny ability to predict what fellow players are likely to do and hence position themselves correctly to intercept the ball (that is they understand how their team-mates construe the situation and hence predict how they will act), but this does not necessarily mean that they understand each other so well off the field.

We so much take it for granted that others are construing our construction of events that deliberate invalidation of the expectations of a character (or indeed of an audience) is a device frequently used by writers of comedy and horror. Tschudi and Rommetveit (1982) quote an example of this from the novel *Blue Movie*. In this Sid Krassman, stepping into a crowded elevator, intones with tremendous authority, 'I suppose you're all wondering why I called you together?' Krassman assumes that the people in the lift construe their all being there together as coincidental, and tries to invalidate their construction by treating them as a group of people called together for a purpose. Milton Erickson (1967) has also deliberately used this technique to overcome people's resistance to hypnotism: having thrown someone's existing construction of the situation into doubt, he found them ready to accept the next one offered. In the lift example what is being invalidated is a socially dominant construction of an event. On other occasions the attempt to invalidate will be based on someone's construction of how a particular individual is construing the situation.

ACTIVITY 5

As you read novels or watch plays on television, make a note of how the author attempts to shock or amuse the audience by deliberately invalidating their expectations.

Are the expectations which have been invalidated cultural ones, or do they depend on understanding how a particular character thinks and feels? You might also want to consider how the effectiveness of this technique might be explained by other psychological theories which you have come across.

PROGRESS BOX

Kelly's personal construct theory is based on a philosophy of *constructive alternativism* – that there are as many ways of construing an event as people can conceive of.

The theory's basic assumption is that each person is a scientist whose *raison d'être* is to develop an increasingly useful model to enable her/him to cope with the world.

The fundamental postulate of personal construct theory – that a person's processes are psychologically channelized by the ways s/he anticipates events – is elaborated in a number of corollaries concerned with aspects such as: construction, dichotomy, organization, individuality, experience, modulation, commonality and sociality.

So far I have taken you on a 'Cook's Tour' of personal construct theory, trying by examples to give you a feel for the way this theory views the world. In the sections which follow I want to look more specifically at how personal construct theory attempts to explain why and how we go about understanding others, but first a detour into methodology.

2 EXPLORING THE CONSTRUCT SYSTEM: THE REPERTORY GRID

In Activity 2 I introduced you to one common way of eliciting constructs but at that time did not give you any indication about how one goes about investigating a person's construct system as a whole. This is very important, however, since – as the organization corollary suggests – it is the ways in which constructs interrelate which best help us to anticipate a person's behaviour.

repertory grid The instrument most closely associated with personal construct theory is the repertory grid or, to give it its full title, the *Role Construct Repertory Test* (grid form). Because Kelly was a clinical psychologist, the grid was initially devised to look at the ways a person construes other people rather than objects. The person whose construct system is being explored is given a set of twenty-four role titles and asked to name the person who fills (or filled) each role in her/his life. For a woman these might include:

(a) the person herself;

(b) members of the family (or those who played a similar role in relation to her), such as mother, stepmother or other person who played a maternal role, brother, or person who was perceived as playing a fraternal role etc.;

(c) people with whom she is at present, or previously had been, intimately associated, such as husband or former boyfriend;

(d) people representing authority, such as a boss or former teacher;

(e) people who arouse a particular emotion, perhaps someone she pitied, or someone who had rejected her;

(f) people who represent valued characteristics – a successful person, a happy person.

These people provide the elements for eliciting constructs and are written along the top of a grid (see Figure 2). The element names are then presented to the person in triads. For each triad she is asked (as described in Activity 2) to think of some important way in which two of the elements are alike, and different from the third. Having elicited a construct on the basis of a particular triad, the person is then asked to apply it to every other element. For instance, suppose the person states that her father and her boss are alike because they 'always know best' (the similarity pole) whereas she is different because she is 'prepared to listen to others' (the difference pole). She is then asked to rate all the elements on the grid, that is family, friends, authority figures etc., as being people who 'always know best' or people who are 'prepared to listen to others'. One common method is for all these elements to be rated on a five-point scale, where those rated '1' are very like the similarity pole (in this case, always know best) and those rated '5' are very like the contrast pole (prepared to listen), the other numbers being applied to elements who are intermediate between the two poles. For example:

1	2	3	4	5
Very much a person who always knows best	Somewhat of a person who always knows best	A person whom one would neither describe as always knowing best or prepared to listen, or who might be both on different occasions	Somewhat a person prepared to listen	Very much a person prepared to listen

1	2	3	4	5	6	7	8	9	10	11	12	13	14	15	16	17	18	19	SORT NO.	EMERGENT POLE	IMPLICIT POLE
					✓		✓		✓							⊗	⊗	○	1	Don't believe in God	Very religious
		✓	✓		✓								⊗	⊗	○			✓	2	Same sort of education	Complete different education
✓		✓	✓	✓	✓			✓	⊗	○	✓	⊗	✓		✓				3	Not athletic	Athletic
	✓		⊗	⊗	○								✓						4	Both girls	A boy
✓	⊗	⊗	○		✓	✓		✓				✓	✓	✓	✓	✓	✓		5	Parents	Ideas different
	✓		○		✓							⊗	✓		⊗				6	Understand me better	Don't understand at all
⊗	✓	✓					○					⊗	✓	✓			✓		7	Teach the right thing	Teach the wrong thing
✓	○	✓											✓	⊗	⊗	✓	✓		8	Achieved a lot	Hasn't achieved a lot
		⊗	✓			✓		○				✓	⊗	✓	✓				9	Higher education	No education
			⊗		✓			⊗	○										10	Don't like other people	Like other people
✓	✓	✓	⊗	✓		✓				○	✓		✓	✓		✓	✓	⊗	11	More religious	Not religious
✓	✓	✓	⊗			✓	✓	○	✓	⊗	✓	✓	✓	✓	✓	✓	✓	✓	12	Believe in higher education	Not believing in too much education
	✓		✓		○				✓	✓	⊗	✓		✓		⊗			13	More sociable	Not sociable
○			⊗	⊗								✓							14	Both girls	Not girls
	✓	○	⊗	⊗								✓							15	Both girls	Not girls
✓	✓	✓	✓	✓			⊗	○				⊗	✓	✓		✓	✓	✓	16	Both have high morals	Low morals
⊗		⊗	○	✓		✓		✓		✓	✓	✓	✓			✓	✓	✓	17	Think alike	Think differently
			✓	✓									✓	⊗	⊗	○	✓		✓	18	Same age	Different ages
	⊗	⊗		✓						✓	○	✓	✓	✓	✓	✓	✓	✓	19	Believe the same about me	Believe differently about me
			✓		✓	⊗	⊗	○	✓	✓	✓	○							20	Both friends	Not friends
				○	✓							⊗	⊗	✓	✓	✓	✓		21	More understanding	Less understanding
⊗		✓		○	✓	⊗						✓			✓		✓		22	Both appreciate music	Don't understand music

Element column headers: 1 Self, 2 Mother, 3 Father, 4 Brother, 5 Sister, 6 Spouse, 7 Ex-flame, 8 Pal, 9 Ex-pal, 10 Rejecting Person, 11 Pitied Person, 12 Threatening Person, 13 Attractive Person, 14 Accepted Teacher, 15 Rejected Teacher, 16 Boss, 17 Successful Person, 18 Happy Person, 19 Ethical Person

Figure 2   An example of a completed role construct repertory test
Source: Kelly, 1955, p. 270

Notes: *'emergent pole'='similarity pole' in the text.
†'implicit pole'='contrast pole' in the text.

Key:
○   Circles indicate the members of the triad on the basis of which the construct was elicited.
⊗⊗   The pair of circles with crosses in are the elements perceived to be similar.
✓   Ticks indicate those elements like the pair.
☐   Blanks are those elements like the remaining person.
(In the grids you will carry out, a five-point rating scale will replace the ticks, crosses and blanks.)

There are other methods for doing these ratings and these are discussed in more detail in the *Kelly Project*. What they all have in common, however, is that they make it possible to see which constructs are being applied similarly by this individual to this set of elements, by using some form of matching score. For example, it may turn out that on the whole, the people she rates as 'always knows best' she also rates as 'rigid', whereas the people who are rated as being 'prepared to listen' are also rated as being 'flexible'. This would indicate that the constructs 'always knows best—prepared to listen' and 'rigid—flexible' are related. Further statistical analyses can then be carried out to determine the main dimensions which underlie the system. (For details see the *Kelly Project*.)

I said above that eliciting the construct system in this way represents the way the person construes one particular set of elements. Care in selecting elements is of the utmost importance in obtaining a useful picture of a construct system. For example, suppose I am interested in how a person construes his friends. If all the elements he uses are close friends, I will get a very different picture from the one I get if he includes people whom he does not like as well as people who are seen as potential friends.

Because my description of the grid was based on Kelly's original repertory test I have been assuming that the elements are different people. That, however, does not need to be the case. Some studies using other kinds of elements are summarized in Box 2 (overleaf).

Box 2 Studies using elements other than individual people

1 Shaw and McKnight (1981) describe a study in which a person chose six roles which he had played in his life. These were: student, teacher, scientist, therapist, father and son. Six grids were then elicited from him using the ARGUS computer program (Shaw, 1980), one from each viewpoint, and using the six roles as elements. So, for example, putting himself in the role of student, he was asked to elicit three constructs using the roles of student, teacher, scientist, therapist, father and son as elements. He was then asked to imagine himself in the next role, in this case as a teacher, and rate the six elements on the constructs elicited so far. Then still in the role of teacher he elicited a new construct which he considered important to that role. The same procedure was followed from the viewpoint of the remaining roles. The results indicated considerable similarity between the grids from the various perspectives, the one which differed most from the others was that elicited in the role of son. The subject commented that when completing this grid he had difficulty in distinguishing between himself as 'son at the present time' and as he had been when an 'adolescent son'.

dyad grid

2 Ryle developed the *dyad grid* (Ryle and Lunghi, 1970; Ryle, 1975) in which the elements are relationships between two persons, for example 'yourself in relation to your father' and 'your father in relation to you'. In eliciting constructs for this type of grid test, elements are presented to subjects in pairs rather than in triads. The following form of elicitation is commonly used: 'Can you tell me ways in which your relationship to your father resembles or differs from your relationship to your mother?' (Ryle, 1975, p. 29). The subject is asked to phrase her/his construct in such a way that it depicts an interaction between two persons. For example, the construct 'exploitative' could take the form *exploits*, or *is exploited by*, so a person might say 'my father exploits me; whereas my mother is exploited by me'. Ryle (1976, p. 71) suggests, 'the dyad form of grid is of particular value where relationships are the main focus of interest, as for example, in the investigation of couples or in the investigation of role relationships' (reported by Adams-Webber, 1979b).

self-identity system

3 Norris and Makhlouf-Norris (1976) investigated the 'self-identity system' by eliciting grids which included among the elements three components of self:

(a) the actual self: being the representation of the person now;

(b) the social self: how the person thinks others see her/him;

(c) the ideal self: how the person would like to be.

The relationship between elements can then be examined to see how the self elements are identified: for example, do I see my actual self as more like my social self or my ideal self, or quite different from them both? In terms of which other elements is the actual/ideal self defined?

3 UNDERSTANDING OTHER PEOPLE: PERSONAL CONSTRUCT THEORY EXPLANATIONS

3.1 Understanding ourselves and others

If one takes a personal construct theory view, it is inevitable that one will be concerned to understand others. After all, the theory postulates that the *raison d'être* of an individual is to understand and cope with the world as effectively as possible, and other people make up a very important part of the world. We therefore must set about trying to make sense of them, or fail disastrously in our life's task.

One of the things we discover fairly quickly is that there are many ways in which other people are similar to us. Presumably, therefore, they are also trying to make sense of what is going on and it might not be a bad idea to join forces. Actually, as you learnt in Block 2, mothers or other caregivers almost from birth set about helping babies to develop their understanding of the world, so the recognition that other people can be helpful in enabling us to cope is probably one of the first things we understand.

According to personal construct theory, if I want to understand a person I must understand how s/he construes the world. I must construe her/his construct system. This is because a person's construct system in a very real way *is* that person. It closely approximates to what in other theories might be called their personality. Kelly does not like to use the term personality, however, because to him it is associated with the idea of something which is largely fixed. In fact, in some theories – such as Eysenck's – personality is seen as genetically based. (For more information on Eysenck's personality theory, see DS 262, Unit 4 (Open University, 1981).) In personal construct theory this is far from the case. Each person is responsible for devising their own construct system and then is capable of changing it. However, we are not normally aware of our construct systems. Many of the discriminations we make have become automatic, some are gut reactions, and many of them do not have verbal labels. So exploring our own construct systems helps to make explicit the guidelines we use in our everyday life. A common reaction of a person seeing the results of their grid is one of surprise: 'Goodness I never knew I saw things that way', they say, 'and yet, when I come to think about it, it makes sense'.

Years ago when I was a school-teacher I elicited a grid on the way I perceived the members of my class. One piece of information that I was confronted with was that those pupils I saw as 'creative' I also saw as 'immature'. This worried me a great deal and led me to try to elaborate my construct of creativity. What was it about immaturity and creativity that made me see them in the same way? Would the relationship between these constructs change if I enlarged my sample of elements to include creative and non-creative adults? Did this relationship mean that as a teacher, presumably encouraging maturity, I was suppressing creativity? Or did I have a view of maturity as solid, rather uninspiring conformity? At the time I elicited this grid my career as a school-teacher was drawing to an end, so constructs relating to me as a teacher were no longer central to my perception of myself and I could envisage changing them. But some constructs are so central to people's view of themselves in relation to others, that the vaguest idea that they might be inadequate is enough to throw them into a state of panic. Look back to the first quotation from Kelly when he is comparing the person's way of developing her/his construct system with that of the scientist. You will notice that he comments, '... both reluctantly revise their predictions in the light of what they observe, on the one hand, and the extent of their theoretical investment, on the other'. Changing central or *core* constructs is a very difficult, and indeed painful, exercise. For example, as a banker's daughter I have had it drummed into me all my life that people who get into debt are untrustworthy. At the same time I have always considered trustworthiness to be of fundamental importance in friendship. Over the years I have discovered that many of the people I consider to be my friends are almost always in debt. There is a mismatch here. These people remain my friends yet display behaviour which I consider untrustworthy. My attempts to reconcile this contradiction lead me to make modifications in my construct system. Perhaps being in debt does not make someone untrustworthy in other ways. Although I cannot necessarily go all the way with them and decide that being in debt is all right, perhaps I can recognize that just because they construe the responsibilities inherent in financial matters differently from the way I do, it does not necessarily imply that their construction of responsibilities in personal relationships is also different. So by trying to construe *their* construct systems rather than assume that they share mine, I am helped to resolve conflicts in my construct system and deepen the basis for my relationships. They also recognize that I use what are, to them, strange ways of construing money. So financial interactions between us are seen by both parties as needing to be handled differently. This is an example of how construing the construction systems of others as described in Kelly's sociality corollary can help both to develop construction systems and to facilitate the growth of friendship.

Let us step back for a while and look at what personal construct theory has to say about the whole process of getting to know people.

3.2   Getting to know people

Because the heart of personal construct theory is the individual construct system, it predicts that people will 'exhibit stable, idiosyncratic preferences for using particular sets of constructs in characterizing themselves and other persons' (Adams-Webber, 1979a, p. 196), and this indeed has been found by people working within the framework of personal construct theory (Bonarius, 1965; Isaacson and Landfield, 1965). There is also evidence, as was suggested earlier, that the constructs people use on first meeting someone are rather different from those they use later in the relationship. An initial meeting can be seen as an opportunity for testing preliminary hypotheses on the basis of which some decisions can be taken about how, or if, the relationship will proceed. But stop a moment. Does this really take place every time you meet someone new?

ACTIVITY 6

Think back over the new people you have met in the last week or so. Does it really make sense to say that you are exploring the possibility of a relationship with all of them?

Unless you are most unusual, this is almost certainly not the case. You will have met a number of people for the first time in a very limited role relationship within which trying to find out how they construe the world would be positively dysfunctional. Imagine the annoyance of the people behind you in the queue if you started to explore the construct system of the post office clerk or the bank teller! In these situations you need only to understand enough of each other's construct systems to ensure that you make the appropriate responses: these will usually involve shared constructions which will not vary much whoever is behind the counter, unless, of course, you are in a foreign country where expectations may be very different, or live in a village or other small community where everyone knows everybody else. Tschudi and Rommetveit (1982) tentatively rephrase Kelly's sociality corollary to take account of this in the following way: '. . . There is an optimal level, depending upon the type of situation, of the extent to which a person should construe the construction process of another in order for maximally viable and efficient social enterprises to take place' (p. 237).

So it seems we need to step back even further and construe the *context* in which the meeting takes place, and this initial construction will determine the constructs you decide are appropriate to the situation. Of course, sometimes this preliminary construal will prove incorrect. Some time ago I stepped out of the front gate of the then new OU London Regional Office to find a police car outside and a policeman looking at the building. My usual constructs about the police led me to wonder what had gone wrong – had there been a burglary, was someone's car badly parked? I had rapidly to reorientate myself when the policeman explained that he was an OU student, that he thought we had met at West Hampstead Study Centre, and then offered me a lift to wherever I was going. I had to stop using constructs to do with behaviour towards people in a policeman role and change to the wider range concerned with behaviour towards OU students.

But supposing you have construed the context in which you are meeting this person for the first time as one in which some longer-term relationship could possibly result. How would personal construct theory explain what goes on?

As a result of experience a person will have built up a set of constructs which s/he has found useful as a means of making decisions about new people. The information initially available will normally be pretty limited: it will usually consist of a limited amount of behavioural data, and information about physical characteristics, mode of dress and so on. Although it seems that young children may actually use physical characteristics as major ways of classifying people (Asch and Nerlove, 1960), as people grow older the significance of even apparently superficial characteristics is likely to have changed. That is to say, when I classify someone as, for example, physically attractive, I will probably not just be making an aesthetic judgement, but will also be tentatively making psychological judgements as well, such as 'Goodness he's goodlooking, probably means he's arrogant and used to getting things his own way'. That is, construing someone in terms of even a fairly superficial characteristic will make a number of different constructions more or less probable. Indeed Duck (1973) found that people produced quite a number of psychological implications from rather superficial constructs, for example, 'wears a suit—does not wear a suit' may imply the psychological construct 'ambitious—not ambitious'.

So far, I have spoken about construing new people almost as if they were objects. I have made it sound as if all that was involved was my observing them and using my observations as the basis for drawing a number of tentative conclusions about them. In fact, what is going on is far more complicated. For example, some of my constructs will take the form of acting in a particular way as an experiment to test my hypotheses about the person concerned: thus, I decide to smile to see whether she will smile back or look away; I crack a joke about the situation to see whether she will laugh or be embarrassed. In other words I act as a scientist. Even more to the point, though, is the fact that while I am doing all these things, the other person will be doing something similar *vis-à-vis* me. In addition to using my own behaviour to test hypotheses about the other, I will also be gathering information from her actions about the sort of person she is and the way she construes me. (This theme is very similar to the 'spiral of perspectives' which is a notion derived from the interactional model discussed in Unit 2.)

What happens as a result of information obtained from the first encounter will depend not only on the information itself but also on other characteristics of the construct system. For example, some people's construct systems will involve a **constellatory constructs** number of what Kelly called constellatory constructs. These are constructs which are tightly clustered, so that if I construe someone as 'x', for instance 'a Tory' or 'a Marxist', then a whole number of other constructs necessarily apply. This is the **stereotypes** kind of construing we use in stereotyping. Such constructs act as very clear, if oversimplified, guides for action. It is possible that for all of us there are some constructs which, if applied to someone, pretty well rule out that person as a potential friend. However, whereas for some people many constructs will act in this way, others will tend to use mainly propositional constructs, that is con- **propositional constructs** structs which 'may be used independently of other ways of understanding an event' (Landfield and Leitner, 1980a). In this case my construing someone as 'a Tory' does not necessarily imply anything else about her to me. Of course, if too many constructs are propositional the person will be left with very little in the way of a guide for action. Perhaps a more useful way of considering initial construing is on a dimension of looseness/tightness: A 'loose' construct is one which can lead to varying predictions but still maintains its identity (Landfield and Leitner, 1980a), so construing a new acquaintance as someone who talks too much leaves open the possibility that he is nervous or domineering, or a bore; 'tight' construing on the other hand leads to unvarying predictions: 'If she is a scientist she *will* be uncultured'.

loose construing

tight construing

According to personal construct theory therefore, the early stages of getting to know someone will depend on the structure and content of both participants' construct systems since these will determine the hypotheses which they bring into a situation and the way in which the information derived from it is used. For example, suppose two people (let's call them Jane and Mary) are meeting for the first time and that Jane has very definite views on the sort of people she is prepared to relate to. To her, if a person shows any signs of being politically right-wing, she rules them out, because in her construct system this also implies that the other person despises anyone who is not successful, and is unfeeling and rigid. Mary, on the other hand, has no such clear ideas. She is not too keen on right-wing people, but her experience has taught her that a person's political views do not necessarily imply anything about other aspects of their personality; indeed in a family crisis it was a Conservative neighbour who lent a hand. What she is much more concerned to find out is whether they are warm, sensitive people, and she will tend to be put off by signs of insensitivity. During their initial interaction, Jane may try to turn the conversation to political issues to discover where Mary stands. Mary can go along with this as the characteristics important to *her* can be demonstrated regardless of the topic being discussed. Jane soon establishes that Mary is not right-wing so is prepared to consider her as a potential friend; Mary is less sure about Jane. There are some indications that although Jane is warm and friendly to people she approves of, she might be rather dismissive of those she does not, so Mary decides to proceed cautiously.

In the terms used above, Jane was using the construct right-wing—left-wing in a constellatory way. If she construed the other person as right-wing, this necessarily implied a whole number of other characteristics which she did not like and this would rule that person out as a potential friend, whereas if she construed them as left-wing, they would necessarily be good. As Mary is left-wing she is all right. As far as Mary is concerned 'left-wing—right-wing' is a propositional construct: that information alone is insufficient to make up her mind about Jane. At this point she leaves her options open. Jane's tight construing leads to clear unvarying predictions; Mary's looser construing leaves open a wider range of possibilities.

Can personal construct theory give us any information about the criteria we will use in deciding whether or not to pursue an acquaintance? Despite the theory's insistence that everyone's construction of reality is different, it appears that it might have some clues to offer. Remember, the aim of everything we do is to help us to understand the world so that we can cope with it better; thus it might be assumed that we will look for relationships which will help us in improving our construction of reality. Perhaps we can get some guidance on how we decide which people will help us most from the 'choice corollary' which says:

choice corollary

> *People choose for themselves that alternative in a dichotomized construct through which they anticipate the greater possibility for the elaboration of their system.*

Elaboration can be of two kinds, either *definition*, which involves more detailed confirmation of some aspect of experience which has already been construed, or *extension*, which is an attempt to explore further areas which are only partly understood. What sort of person can be expected to help in this elaboration? In the first place it will be difficult to cooperate with someone unless we have some shared frame of reference within which to work. If the other person's construct system is so different from mine that I am quite unable to make any sense of it, I will feel so threatened by my inability to cope, that cooperation with that person will be impossible. No extension of my construction system will be possible there. In McCoy's (1977) work on 'foreign' wives in Hong Kong, she finds evidence to support a theory put forward by Adler (1975) that after an initial stage of excitement and enthusiasm for the new culture, people suffer a period during which they become aware of the 'inadequacy of their construct system in the face of new and unconstrued events, as well as awareness of the deficiencies of predictions from the old construct system' (1980, p. 145). At this stage the new culture is perceived as so threatening that people may withdraw completely from contact or construe it in such a negative way as to make it not worth bothering about and hence the threat is modified. Until this stage is passed, elaboration of the construct system so as to be able to cope with the new events will be impossible.

From this it seems probable that the people we will seek out will be those we construe as reasonably similar to ourselves as they will be seen as offering us the possibility for improved definition of our construct system. This means that we must first of all find out whether or not they are sufficiently similar. It is not enough for us actually to be similar: that is, commonality alone is not enough; we must *construe* each other's construct systems as similar. It would, however, appear likely that the existence of commonality (similar construction of experience) would make it easier for people to understand each other (to construe each other's construction).

Box 3 Similarity of construing and friendship

There is some evidence to support the view that initial similarity of construing is related to subsequent friendship (Duck, 1973). Sixteen new female students of geography living in the same hall of residence were asked to complete a repertory grid of 16 elements, which were people playing specified roles in their lives. About six months later they completed a second smaller repertory grid on which the first six role titles were the same as on the previous occasion and the last six were '(7) self, (8) someone you dislike, (9) someone you admire, (10, 11, 12) three personal friends' (p. 156). At the same time a list of friendship choices was obtained using a sociometric technique. This is a technique for collecting information about interpersonal choices by means of a questionnaire which asks the subject to name the person who best fits a particular preference criterion: for instance, with whom would you most like to work?; to whom would you most like to spend an evening talking?, and so on. A comparison of the verbal construct labels for similarity between friendship and non-friendship pairs showed that girls who subsequently became friends showed greater similarity of construing on the first test than did the other pairs.

sociometric technique

Much evidence (Piaget, 1926; Flavell, 1968) suggests that young children initially assume that everyone sees things the same way that they do. Learning that this is not so may be a long process because sometimes this assumption works. 'For instance, a young child may correctly predict another child's feelings in a situation with which he is familiar. What he may in fact have done is to simply state what he felt in that familiar situation, which coincidently predicts correctly what the other child feels' (Gruen and Doherty (1977) reported by Hayden, 1982). At other times this will not work and invalidation will occur. With increasing invalidations, the child will learn that it is necessary to understand something about a person (to construe their constructions) in order to have a reasonable chance of predicting correctly what they will do.

People increasingly learn more about each other's construct systems, including, of course, their constructions of each other. Duck (1973) has suggested that in forming and maintaining relationships we are seeking for validation (and I would add elaboration) of our own constructions. He has provided evidence for this by showing that people are more likely to use constructs similar to those of their friends than those of non-friends. It might be interesting to take this further and hypothesize that our friends will construe us as we would wish to be construed, thus validating the valued aspects of our self-construction and providing personality support (as I suggested earlier).

Much of what is going on in relationships can be seen as involving testing the adequacy of our construction of the other and the acceptability or otherwise of their construction of us. The first time I invite a new acquaintance to join me in some activity, or to meet other friends, I am testing out my hypothesis about what s/he likes doing, or the sort of people s/he will find interesting. Choosing gifts can also be seen as evidence of a person's ability and/or desire to construe other people's construction systems adequately. For some people the choice of gifts is based only on the need for it to be not widely inappropriate – whereas for others, choice of a personally appropriate gift is a way of showing that you understand their likes and dislikes, and that you care sufficiently about them to want to get it right. The fact that small children often choose as presents things which they want themselves confirms the slow development of sociality. Flavell (1968) found evidence of an increase with age of children's ability to choose sex- and age-appropriate gifts.

Understanding other people's construct systems makes it possible to manage our relationships more effectively. You can recognize areas where you construe things differently from someone else and may choose whether or not to talk about them, depending on the cost and possible gain to the relationship. If it is the case that one chooses to pursue relationships with those who validate and perhaps elaborate our construct systems, it seems likely that it will be the validation of core constructs which will be crucial in determining intimacy, close friends being those with whom central experiences can be shared without fear of invalidation. However, quite satisfactory relationships may exist with people who construe a number of less central issues similarly, for example people who share some of the same interests.

4   PERSONAL CONSTRUCT THEORY: SOME CRITICISMS

In this section I want to examine some of the criticisms of personal construct theory which you will come across. They seem to me to be of three distinct types: those which arise from the varying views which people have of the function of psychological theories; those which stem either from an inadequate understanding of the theory, or from identifying the theory too closely with the repertory grid method; and lastly I shall outline some criticisms which must be taken into account in future developments of the theory.

Sometimes a theory may be criticized for not doing something which in fact it never had any intention of doing. Such criticisms question the philosophical assumptions underlying the theory, for instance, 'Personal construct theory does not lead to the discovery of general (or universal) laws about human nature', or 'It does not take into account biological factors underlying human behaviour', or 'It does not use operational definitions'.

Differing views on the functions of theories in psychology are discussed in the Metablock and I suggest you look at paper 2 in Part III now.

A second type of criticism stems either from an inadequate understanding of the theory, or from identifying the theory too closely with the method of repertory grid techniques. The three most common criticisms are set out below.

(a)   'Personal construct theory is too cognitive; it ignores the emotions.'

It has been usual for psychologists to categorize experience as either cognitive or emotional, rational or irrational, frequently assuming a close relationship between the cognitive and the rational on the one hand and the emotional and irrational on the other. Kelly says that this has become 'a barrier to sensitive psychological enquiry' (Kelly, 1979), that it prevents the study of the 'whole person'.

If you stop and think about it, few if any of our experiences can be said to be completely cognitive or completely emotional. As I struggle to rewrite this Unit in the light of people's comments I can be said to be performing a cognitive task but I am far from devoid of emotions – excitement at a new idea, boredom with writing a passage for the fourth time, irritation with a colleague's failure to understand. Many, if not all, of the constructs I use to make sense of what is going on are suffused with emotion. Can the constructs 'love—hate' or 'friendly—unfriendly' ever be considered purely cognitive?

Kelly does deal with a small set of emotions by name and these he defines in such a way as 'to enable a therapist to construe another's behaviour in a therapeutically useful manner' (McCoy, 1977). So, for example, 'the immediate cause of anxiety is not an external stimulus such as a knock on the door by the bill collector or a "Dear John" letter. Rather it is the internal phenomenon, the recognition of the impact of a prediction one makes regarding the self in these circumstances' (ibid., p. 77). The debt collector's arrival thus threatens my construction of myself as trustworthy in money matters; receipt of the 'Dear John' letter may threaten the recipient's construction of himself as deserving love.

(b)   'Constructs are "black-and-white affairs" and oversimplify experience.'

I have tried to forestall this criticism in my discussion of the dichotomy corollary, but as it is one of the most frequent criticisms of personal construct theory, it is important to include it here. I suggest you look back to the earlier discussion now.

(c)   'Personal construct theory is too static.'

I think this derives from the mistaken view that the grid reveals the whole construct system, rather than being a 'snapshot' of a section of the construct system *at a particular time*. Closer examination of the experience, modulation and choice corollaries should help dispense with this criticism, as should Kelly's explicit statement that the focus of convenience of the theory is the 'reconstruction of life' (Kelly, 1955).

There are other criticisms which need to be taken into account in future developments of personal construct theory.

(a)   'Personal construct theory is too heavily individualistic.'

Kelly did not intend to produce a purely individualistic theory. In fact at one point, he considered calling it 'role theory' and considered the sociality corollary to be at the heart of the theory and to have the most far-reaching implications. It is perhaps because an approach which was centrally concerned with the individual's construction of the world was so different from the psychological approaches current at the time, and that the apparent precision of the repertory grid enabled psychologists not to stray too far from the fold of quantitative analysis, that individuals' construct systems became the focus of research to the neglect of sociality. At the present time a number of attempts are being made to redress the balance. This is exemplified by the publication in 1979 of *Constructs of Sociality and Individuality*, edited by Bannister and Stringer, and the work of Steve Duck which is referred to throughout the Block. At the same time the growth of computer techniques for eliciting and analysing repertory grids makes it easier to study sociality. One of the project options which will be offered in some years to people doing the Kelly Project will give you the chance to discover how well you are able to construe someone else's construction system.

(b) 'Personal construct theory pays insufficient attention to the part played by the wider social context in the development of constructs.'

This criticism can be made at two levels. First it can be seen as a criticism of the theory itself in that it does not take account of the social and psychological environment from which it emerged. As Holland (1970, 1981) states, 'Personal construct theory lacks an awareness of the processes of knowledge production.' Kelly himself fails to refer or link to, except in a rather disparaging way, the major psychological theories of his time and he does not show an awareness of the influences of the prevailing ideology. If the theory is to reach its full potential, Holland argues it will need to 'apply to itself all the resources of sociopsychological analysis in deep self-criticism' (1981, p. 28).

Secondly, it can be seen as a criticism of the theory's failure to pay sufficient attention to the role played by the social context in the individual's construction of reality. Kelly was aware of cultural influences on people's construing as can be seen in some of his accounts of clinical work (Kelly, 1955, Vol. 2). His insistence that it is the way each person *construes* her/his circumstances which is of importance can lead us to fail to consider the extent to which living in a particular cultural context directs our attention to some aspects of the world rather than others. Greater attention to the social influences on people's construing could do much to improve the status of personal construct theory as a social psychological theory.

Review of objectives

As is usual with Open University Units, I started this one by setting out the objectives which it was designed to achieve. Now I have reached the end it is time to look back and see to what extent they have been achieved.

1   Describe the main principles of personal construct theory.

This is the substance of section 1.

2   Understand the philosophy underlying the theory and the methodology associated with it.

The philosophy underlying personal construct theory is one of constructive alternativism epitomized in Kelly's statement that 'the events we face today are subject to as great a variety of constructions as our wits will enable us to contrive' (1970, p. 1). This is discussed at the beginning of section 1, where reference is also made to the model of the person as a lay scientist trying to make sense of the world in order to be able to cope with it better. Section 2 provides a brief description of the repertory grid, which is the method most closely associated with Kelly. There are a number of less formal methods which have not been discussed. You will find it useful to bear in mind the basis of Kelly's approach when you come to study other approaches to understanding other people which are discussed in this Block.

3   Understand how the construct system of the individual influences the way s/he perceives and relates to others.

This is the core of section 3, but the various examples throughout the earlier sections are also intended to help you achieve this objective.

4   Recognize that this is a dynamic and interactive process.

Personal construct theory is about making hypotheses and testing them out, as the fundamental postulate states. The construct system changes with experience (experience corollary) through *modulation* and *making* choices. We come to understand others by sociality, construing the construction systems of others, part of which is the other person's construct of us.

5   Evaluate the contribution of personal construct theory in explaining how people understand others.

To some extent this objective requires you to look forward to the rest of the Block and see whether your understanding of personal construct theory helps you to explain the evidence provided there. The hypothesis that we develop relationships with people who validate our construct systems (proposed by Duck) has begun to be explored here. How well does it help you to make sense of your relationships?

6   Explore your own construct system and try to understand how it is similar to or different from others'.

Section 2 and the Activities should help you begin to do this. This objective will be best achieved if you carry out the Kelly Project.

References

ADAMS-WEBBER, J.R. (1979a) 'Construing persons in social contexts', in Stringer, P. and Bannister, D. (eds) (1979).

ADAMS-WEBBER, J. R. (1979b) *Personal Construct Theory: Concepts and Applications*, London, John Wiley and Sons.

ADLER, P. S. (1975) 'The transitional experience: an alternative view of culture shock', *Journal of Humanistic Psychology*, Vol. 15, pp. 13–23.

ASCH, S. E. and NERLOVE, O. (1960) 'The development of double function terms in children', in Kaplan, B. and Wapner, S. (eds) (1960) *Perspectives in Psychological Theory*, New York, International University Press.

BANNISTER, D. (ed.) (1970) *Perspectives in Personal Construct Theory*, London, Academic Press.

BANNISTER, D. and MAIR, J. M. M. (eds) (1968) *Evaluation of Personal Constructs*, London, Academic Press.

BONARIUS, J. C. J. (1965) 'Research in the personal construct theory of George A Kelly', in Maher, B. A. (ed.) *Progress in Experimental Personality Theory*, Vol. 2, London, Academic Press.

BONARIUS, H., HOLLAND, R. and ROSENBERG, S. (eds) (1981) *Personal Construct Theory: Recent Advances in Theory and Practice*, London, Macmillan.

BROWN, R. (1965) *Social Psychology*, New York, The Free Press.

CLARK, R. A. and DELIA, J. G. (1976) 'The development of functional persuasive skills in childhood and early adolescence', *Child Development*, Vol. 47, pp. 1008–14.

COONEY, E. W. and SELMAN, R. L. (1978) 'Children's use of social conceptions', in Darwen, W. (ed.) *Social Cognition*, San Francisco, Jossey-Bass.

DUCK, S. W. (1973) *Personal Relationships and Personal Constructs: A Study of Friendship Formation*, London, John Wiley and Sons.

DUCK, S. W. (1975) 'Personality similarity and friendship choices by adolescents', *European Journal of Social Psychology*, Vol. 5, pp. 70–83.

EPTING, F. R. (1984) *Personal Construct Counseling and Psychotherapy*, London, John Wiley and Sons.

ERICKSON, M. H. (1967) 'Advanced techniques of hypnosis and therapy', in Haley, J. (ed.) *Selected Papers of Milton H. Erickson, M.D.*, New York, Grune and Stratton.

FLAVELL, J. H. (1968) *The Development of Role-taking and Communication Skills in Children*, London, John Wiley and Sons.

GRUEN, G. and DOHERTY, J. (1977) 'A constructivist view of major development shifts in early childhood', in Uzgiris, C. and Weizmann, F. (eds) *The Structuring of Experience*, New York, Plenum Press.

HAYDEN, D. C. (1982) 'Experience – a case for possible change: the modulation corollary', in Marcuse, J. E. and Adams-Webber, J. R. (eds) (1982).

HINKLE, D. N. (1965) 'The change of personal constructs from the viewpoint of a theory of implications', unpublished PhD thesis, Ohio State University.

HOLLAND, R. (1970) 'George Kelly: constructive innocent and reluctant existentialist', in Bannister, D. (ed.) (1970).

HOLLAND, R. (1981) 'From perspectives to reflectivity', in Bonarius, H. *et al.* (eds) (1981).

ISAACSON, G. I. and LANDFIELD, A. W. (1965) 'The meaningfulness of personal and common constructs', *Journal of Individual Psychology*, Vol. 21, pp. 160–6.

KELLY, G. A. (1955) *The Psychology of Personal Constructs*, Vols 1 and 2, New York, Norton.

KELLY, G. A. (1970) 'A brief introduction to personal construct theory', in Bannister, D. (ed.) (1970).

KELLY, G. A. (1979) 'Humanistic methodology in psychological research', in Maher, B. (ed.) (1979) *Clinical Psychology and Personality: The Selected Papers of George Kelly*, New York, Krieger.

KELLY, G. A. (1980) 'The psychology of optimal man', in Landfield, A. W. and Leitner, L. M. (eds) (1980b).

LANDFIELD, A. W. and LEITNER, L. M. (1980a) 'Personal construct psychology', in Landfield, A. W. and Leitner, L. M. (eds) (1980b).

LANDFIELD, A. W. and LEITNER, L. M. (eds) (1980b) *Personal Construct Psychology: Psychotherapy and Personality*, London, John Wiley and Sons.

LITTLE, B. R. (1968) 'Factors affecting the use of psychological versus non-psychological constructs on the rep test', *Bulletin of the British Psychological Society*, Vol. 21, No. 70, p. 34.

MARCUSE, J. C. and ADAMS-WEBBER, J. R. (eds) (1982) *The Construing Person*, New York, Praeger.

McCOY, M. (1977) 'A reconstruction of emotion', in Bannister, D. (ed.) (1977) *New Perspectives in Personal Construct Theory*, London, Academic Press.

McCOY, M. (1980) 'Culture-shocked marriages', in Landfield, A. W. and Leitner, L. M. (eds) (1980b).

McCOY, M. (1981) 'Personal construct theory and methodology in intercultural research', paper presented at the Fourth International Congress on Personal Construct Psychology, St. Catherines, Ontario.

NORRIS, H. and MAKHLOUF-NORRIS, F. (1976) 'The measurement of self-identity', in Slater, P. (ed.) (1976).

OPEN UNIVERSITY (1981) DS 262 *Introduction to Psychology*, Unit 4 'Dimensions of personality' by Steve Blinkhorn, Milton Keynes, The Open University Press.

PIAGET, J. (1926) *The Language and Thought of the Child*, New York, Harcourt Brace Jovanovich.

PIAGET, J. (1932) *The Moral Judgement of the Child*, London, Routledge and Kegan Paul.

ROSS, L. (1981) 'The "intuitive scientist" formulation and its developmental implications', in Flavell, J. H. and Ross, L. (eds) (1981) *Social Cognitive Development: Frontiers and Possible Futures*, Cambridge, Cambridge University Press.

RYLE, A. (1975) *Frames and Cages: The Repertory Grid Approach to Human Understanding*, Falmer, University of Sussex Press.

RYLE, A. (1976) 'Some clinical application of grid technique', in Slater, P. (ed.) (1976).

RYLE, A. and LUNGHI, M. W. (1970) 'The dyad grid: a modification of repertory grid technique', *British Journal of Psychiatry*, Vol. 117, pp. 323–7.

SHAW, M. L. G. (1980) *On Becoming a Personal Scientist: Interactive Computer Elicitation of Personal Models of the World*, London, Academic Press.

SHAW, M. L. G. and McKNIGHT, C. (1981) 'ARGUS: a program to explore intrapersonal personalities', in Shaw, M. L. G. (ed.) *Recent Advances in Personal Construct Technology*, London, Academic Press.

SLATER, P. (ed.) (1976) *Explorations of Intrapersonal Space*, Vol. 1, London, John Wiley and Sons.

STRINGER, P. and BANNISTER, D. (eds) (1979) *Constructs of Sociality and Individuality*, London, Academic Press.

TSCHUDI, F. and ROMMETVEIT, R. (1982) 'Sociality, intersubjectivity, and social processes: the sociality corollary', in Marcuse, J. C. and Adams-Webber, J. R. (eds) (1982).

TYLER, M. (1981) 'Kelly's "road to freedom"? Problems in understanding the process of construct system development', in Bonarius, H. *et al.* (eds) (1981).

WEEKS, D. R. (1972) *A Glossary of Sociological Concepts*, Milton Keynes, The Open University Press.

Acknowledgements

Grateful acknowledgement is made to the following sources for material used in this Unit:

Table 1 from S. W. Duck, *Personal Relationships and Personal Constructs: A Study of Friendship Formation*, © 1973, reprinted by permission of John Wiley and Sons, Inc.; *Figure 1* by kind permission of Dr William H. Ittelson; *Figure 2* from George A. Kelly, *The Psychology of Personal Constructs*, Vol. 1, New York, W. W. Norton and Company Inc., copyright © George A. Kelly, 1955.

Index of concepts

UNIT 9
UNDERSTANDING OTHERS II: THE APPROACH OF ATTRIBUTION THEORY

Prepared for the course team by Charles Antaki

CONTENTS

Objectives

After reading this Unit you should be able to:

1 Appreciate the difficulties facing a psychology of ordinary explanations.

2 Understand how experimental social psychology has simplified explanations into manageable concepts.

3 Describe the main attributional models and how the models of Jones and Davis, of Kelley, and of Jones and Nisbett differ from one another.

4 Evaluate the evidence for the actor-observer difference in attributions and for the existence of a self-serving bias in attributions.

5 Know how you could apply what you have learned in this Unit to your *own* explanations of social behaviour.

Study guide

This Unit is about how you and I try to understand and explain the actions of the people around us. The theories presented in this Unit share several common assumptions with personal construct theory, but you should be clear at the outset about two major differences:

(a) personal construct theory focuses on the *individual,* and her/his own particular set of beliefs about the world, whereas attribution theories are more concerned with the *general* rules of how we explain the reasons for other people's actions;

(b) the degree of emphasis on the interpersonal context is different: attribution theories are explicitly concerned with explaining the actions of another person during interactions, which is necessarily a *relational* approach; personal construct theory focuses much more on describing the *individual's* model of the world (which will, of course, involve other people).

ordinary explanations Attempts made by any of us to understand the actions of those with whom we interact are called 'ordinary explanations' to distinguish them from the psychologist's theories about actions. One of the major psychological theories about these ordinary explanations is called 'attribution theory' and it is this theory (in several versions) which will form the focus for this Unit.

Set reading

The following paper will need to be read during your work on section 3:

M. Lalljee (1981) 'Attribution theory and the analysis of explanations', in Antaki, C. (ed.) (1981) *The Psychology of Ordinary Explanations of Social Behaviour,* New York and London, Academic Press, Ch. 5, pp. 119-38. This is reprinted in the *Offprints Booklet.*

1 PERCEIVING THE CAUSES OF BEHAVIOUR

My next-door-neighbour always invites his friends round late at night, especially his girlfriend, and they are noisy. They're always opening the doors and moving the furniture about.

There isn't any real explanation for what they do. That is why it is so annoying. I think they are usually drunk and need to go to the toilet a lot. The girlfriend probably can't help the way she is. I don't usually try to explain there [sic] actions I just think they are a pair of creeps anyway. He is in the folkclub and has a lot of musical equipment I think he takes it down to the music room a lot that may explain some of the noises. The girlfriend thinks he is witty which is probably why she is always laughing. I think they are both childish.

(University student in a hall of residence)

How does this student come to make these statements? He claims that he does not think 'there is any real explanation' for what his neighbours do, but then he goes ahead and gives several anyway – some neutral, but most rather negative. In this section we shall try to discover what sort of information the student has based his explanation on, how that information is processed, and what importance it might have in his social life.

There are many ways in which psychologists might tackle this question. One important (early) tradition has been to consider what impressions people form of other people when they first encounter them. This investigation of first impressions is known as 'person perception'.

person perception

1.1 Person perception: the perception of outward appearance and inner characteristics

A great deal of social psychological theory in the 1950s and 1960s was devoted to uncovering the processes by which we 'see' others, and on what we base our impressions of them. How do we infer inner characteristics from outward appearances? How do we infer that someone is intelligent or a 'happy sort of person' from photographs? What do we conclude from descriptions of personality? How are we influenced by external factors like knowing a person's job?

Person perception theories were concerned with how people coped with descriptions of others. A classic experiment – outlined in Box 1 – illustrates what I mean.

Box 1   The work of Asch on impression formation

Asch's (1946) work concerned the perception of other people *(targets)* described by lists of personality trait adjectives. For instance, in one study he asked his subjects to rate an individual who was described as either:

intelligent	or:	intelligent
skilful		skilful
industrious		industrious
warm		cold
determined		determined
practical		practical
cautious		cautious

---

independent variable

dependent variable

By comparing the subjects' responses to the two descriptions, Asch was able to assess the impact of the trait 'warm – cold' (the only different trait on the two lists). Perhaps surprisingly, the impact of this independent variable (that is, an identifiable factor which was manipulated in the experiment) was extensive and affected subjects' ratings of the target's happiness, popularity, generosity and shrewdness, amongst other things. (These ratings or measurements made in an experiment are called the dependent variables.) Asch argued that people have systematic processes of cognitive organization underlying the formation of such impressions from collections of traits, and that some traits are more important influences upon such organization (*central* traits) than others (which he termed *peripheral* traits). Thus the dimension 'warm – cold' was central, and fundamentally affected the impressions formed by his subjects of the target.

Asch was concerned with the ways in which people *combine* information presented to them and he identified the overriding effects of particular sorts of traits upon the impressions which individuals formed. However, criticism was levelled at his experiments for being too removed from how we form impressions about people in 'real life', rather than just responding to written adjective lists. Harold Kelley (1950) looked at how influential these effects were in real social situations: how he did this is shown in Box 2. (Do not confuse Harold Kelley with George Kelly whose personal construct theory you met in the last Unit.)

Box 2   The work of Kelley on impression formation

Kelley's (1950) experiment was designed to study the combined effects of a *description* of a person in trait adjective terms, with the *experience* of her/his actions in real life. Students who were to hear a lecture were handed a paper with descriptions of the lecturer who would give it. Half of the students received one description of the lecturer and half of them another which differed in one key phrase ('rather cold' versus 'very warm'). The description was:

> 'Mr – is a graduate student in the Department of Economics and Social Science here at MIT. He has three semesters of teaching experience at another college. This is his fifth semester teaching [this course]. He is twenty-six years old, a [Vietnam] veteran, and married. People who know him consider him to be a rather cold (/ very warm) person, industrious, critical, practical and determined.'

You can see that once again, the key independent variable in the study was the manipulation of the 'warm – cold' dimension. The lecturer then entered and delivered the lecture. It was, of course, precisely the same lecture for each person there, in content and presentation, but Kelley was interested to see how the pre-information influenced subjects' perceptions of the performance and the performer. The 'warm' subjects later rated the lecturer as more considerate of others, more informal, more sociable, more popular, better natured, more humorous and more humane than the 'cold' subjects. Thus the Kelley experiment is largely supportive of Asch's findings that prior expectations influence the perception of real persons.

Considerable work in this area has been done since these studies were performed, particularly on the question of the influence of such impressions on actual social behaviour during interactions with the person who has been judged. It seems fairly clear from this work that the formation of impressions based on prior expectations is extremely relevant to the actual formation of social relationships.

The work of Asch and Kelley examined how individuals form impressions once the information has been selected, but we may also expect there to be differences in the ways in which people select this information about people they meet. Kaplan (1973) showed that impressions are influenced by one's own initial disposition or tendencies to evaluate others in either a positive or negative manner. Such dispositions clearly exist *before* we receive any information about the other person, and as such they reflect our tendencies towards affiliation and liking for other people which pre-exist our meetings with them. Some people always seem able to see any individual they meet as likeable and enjoyable, whilst others seem to see everyone they meet in a negative way. Will Rogers, the American cowboy-philosopher, is reported to have claimed that he never met a person he did not like, whilst it is clear that Ebeneezer Scrooge, in Charles Dickens' *A Christmas Carol*, tended to evaluate everyone negatively and to be highly suspicious and vigilant about their true motives.

Person perception and impression formation research told us much about what information people used in their perceptions of others. But in 1958 Heider set off a new stream of thought in social psychology by asking the fundamental question – how do people understand others' actions? He moved the spotlight away from people's perception of others' traits and static qualities and onto people's perception of the *causes* of others' actions.

If we go back to the example at the beginning of the section, we see that our student subject may or may not have been reporting his perception of his neighbour on the basis of his static, visible qualities; but what he was certainly doing was explaining his *actions*. Heider alerted social psychologists to the simple, well-observed fact that all of us, at least some of the time, consciously try to explain to ourselves the *reasons* for other people's actions. All of us, in every social interaction, need to have at least some idea of what it is the other person is up to. What are these 'reasons' we attribute to others? What are these unconscious theories or conscious ideas we have about other people, and how do we arrive at them?

1.1.1 The ordinary explainer's search for the causes of behaviour

In the 1940s Heider had already done work that suggested to him that social perception (that is, the way we see others) is driven by the desire to know what causes things to happen. In an early experiment (Heider and Simmel, 1944) he showed people a film of animated geometrical shapes simply moving about the screen. He had so arranged these movements that the shapes appeared to move in relation to each other. His subjects reported what they did in anthropomorphic terms, saying that the circle was 'following' the square, the triangle was 'chasing' the circle, and so on. This use of purposive terms and the implication that one shape's behaviour caused another to change struck Heider as a symptom of our *fundamental search for causation* in the moving world around us.

Heider used this simple observation as a basic assumption of his approach to social psychology. He made the point that if people explain the movement of geometric shapes by attributing to them wants and desires and intentions, then they will, in all probability, be doing the same in their explanations of the actions of people. Further, if they (that is, we) explain other people's actions by attributing what they do to *internal* causes such as their wants, needs and intentions, then it is likely that there exists a potentially complementary set of *external* causes. These were what Heider called environmental causes – things to do with the circumstances or situations in which the action was performed. From the point of view of the development of social psychology, one of Heider's major contributions was to divide the potential sources of actions into two: personal (internal/dispositional) causes and environmental (external/situational) causes.

internal (personal) causes
external (environmental) causes

attribution theory

According to Heider, the job of the ordinary explainer is to decide whether a given action springs from something within the person who is performing it, or from outside, environmental pressure. This was, and still is, the core of attribution theory.

Two major models which have been derived from Heider's original work are discussed in this section. The first to be described, the correspondent inference model, assumes that the ordinary explainer wants to infer an internal disposition to her/his partner which *corresponds* with (and thus explains) the partner's actions, ignoring possible external causes. In the second model, the covariance model, the explainer is assumed to be more open-minded about what would count as an explanation of the performer's actions and so allows the explainer to reach the conclusion that the actions might be caused by the performer's circumstances *or* by an internal disposition. The correspondent inference model treats the circumstances as an impediment to an explanation, rather than a substantial explanation in their own right.

Further comparisons of the models are presented after both models have been described.

1.2 Jones and Davis' model of correspondent inferences

The first psychologists to take Heider's principles and turn them into a formal theory of explanations were Edward E. Jones and Keith Davis (Jones and Davis, 1965). They made the observation that people often explain someone's actions by saying that they are due to their personality (or, in Jones and Davis' language, to

dispositions
dispositional attribution
their dispositions). A disposition is a relatively long-standing trait or characteristic. So a dispositional attribution is the attribution of the cause of someone's actions to some internal, enduring characteristic. As psychologists, Jones and Davis pointed out that this is often a mistaken explanation of why people act as they do. But they noted that, though mistaken, it is a usefully lazy kind of explanation. It means that the explainer has a ready-made cause to explain her/his friends' actions – the explainer could just say 'Well, that's the way they are', describing them as a 'pair of creeps' perhaps, as our student did. But why do people tend to make this type of dispositional attribution? Jones and

correspondent inference model
Davis proposed a theory of 'correspondent inferences' to account for this, where a person *infers* a disposition in another person which *corresponds* to her/his actions.

The first assumption that the explainer makes, according to this theory, is that the other person (the 'performer') *intended* and *knew* what s/he was doing (the

knowledge criterion
ability criterion
knowledge criterion), and the second is that the behaviour was not just the result of blind chance (the ability criterion). Once these two assumptions are made, the explainer then imagines what alternatives were open to the performer. If there were none, then the performer may simply have *had* to do what he did, *or* s/he may have chosen to do so because of an internal disposition; we just cannot tell.

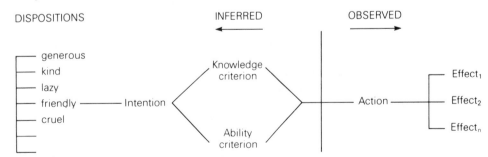

Figure 1 Attribution of dispositions from observed actions
Source: Jones and Davis, 1965

Figure 1 is to be read from *right to left*. On the right are the *observed effects* that the performer intended (we assume) to bring about by performing a particular action. What we have to do is *infer* a disposition *corresponding* to that action.

How do we make that inference? Let us see with the aid of an example.

A colleague from work whom you know slightly invites you to her house for a meal. She and her husband are good conversationalists and the evening passes well. The centrepiece is a very elaborate and obviously expensive meal. You do not comment on it at the time, but on the way back home you puzzle over it. She has gone to a great deal of trouble and also expense to present something impressive. This is the 'action' we have to explain. Is it due to a disposition of hers to 'be like that', or is there some other explanation?

To answer this question, Jones and Davis say that what we do is first think of what she might have done (what other actions she might have taken) and what the *effects* of those actions would have been. Let us take our example through these next two steps. We shall assume only *one* other action – that she cooked a plain meal. Underneath the two actions you can see the *effects* listed. Examine the first pair of effects.

	Impressive meal	*Straightforward meal*	
common effect	everyone is adequately fed	everyone is adequately fed	*common effect*

The first effect is common to both alternatives, so is uninformative for us as it does not distinguish between them. Next we find that the effects differ in how much they are to be enjoyed by the guests:

	Impressive meal	*Straightforward meal*	
	everyone is adequately fed	everyone is adequately fed	
non-common effect	everyone relishes the food	—	*non-common effect*

This non-common effect discriminates between the two alternatives, but since any host or hostess would want their guests to relish the food, we cannot make a very confident inference about her dispositions yet. We proceed in our mulling over and find that there *is* something that is a non-common effect and is also unlikely to have been done out of a sense of duty:

	Impressive meal	*Straightforward meal*	
	everyone is adequately fed	everyone is adequately fed	
uninformative non-common effect	guests relish the food	—	*uninformative non-common effect*
informative non-common effect	guests are ostentatiously entertained	—	*informative non-common effect*

generally undesirable effect

We assume that not all hosts would want their guests to feel deliberately and ostentatiously entertained (in Jones and Davis' terms, that ostentation is a generally undesirable effect), so we feel that it must reflect a true inner disposition on her part, a liking for ostentation and show. Perhaps her norms and etiquette are different from ours; anyway, we are relatively confident in now thinking of her as a showy person.

According to Jones and Davis, then, ordinary explanation of people's actions proceeds by listing what the effects of their actions will be and finding expected effects that one choice has that the others do not (the non-common effects). Then you calculate whether those non-common effects would be generally desirable or undesirable. The *less* non-common effects there are and the *less* generally desirable we think they are (fairly undesirable in our hypothetical case), then the *more* we can draw a correspondent inference between the effect and the disposition we think caused it.

How do you think the model copes with those everyday situations where there are many non-common effects between many alternatives? Is it the case that we simply have no confident explanation about what made a person act as s/he did?

According to Jones and Davis, what we do when we are faced with a multitude of non-common effects is to rate each one for the probability it *generally* has of causing someone to act in that way. Take as an example the case of your neighbours using a small win on a lottery to buy a dinghy. Why might they have done this? Jones and Davis would say that we ought to think of all the likely things that the neighbours *could* have done with the money, list their non-common effects and rate these for social undesirability. For example, we could say that they could have used the money to patch up the windows, and having a damp house is generally undesirable, so not choosing to repair the windows must mean they really do have a strong liking for dinghy sailing.

This is not an entirely satisfactory solution to the problem of what to do when there are many non-common effects between the alternatives of a person's actions, and we shall return to this and other questions we might pose about the model in section 1.2.3.

Let us continue now by noting that so far we have talked about how people rather neutrally explain the actions of other people. In the exercises above, we could look at all the evidence coolly and make a dispassionate judgement about their reasons at our leisure; their actions did not have any immediate significance for us, we were not likely to be pushed or pulled in any way by any biases or worries we may have had about their actions. But personal involvement in others' actions *does* play a part in how we see them, and Jones and Davis make room for such an **hedonic relevance** effect in their model. They call it the effect of 'hedonic relevance' of the action to the perceiver. If I was a perceiver of someone else's action, I would be influenced in how I saw *what* he did – as would my perceptions of the *reasons* for what he did – by how the outcomes of his action affected me.

Take the case of someone whose actions determine not only *her* fate but also her colleagues' – someone on an assembly line for example. If she makes a mistake or stops the machine, the effect travels all the way down and everyone 'downstream' from her suffers. If these workers were on piece-rates this could have direct and unwelcome effects on their wage-packet, and thus might affect their explanation of what happened. Box 3 outlines an experiment which shows this effect.

Box 3   Hedonic relevance

A version of this scenario was set up in a laboratory by Jones and DeCharms (1957). Two groups of subjects were formed, both of which had to work on a common task, and both of which had a confederate of the experimenter as a member of the group. One group was told that they would only get rewarded if *everyone* succeeded on the task (so each person's actions had high hedonic relevance for everyone else) while the other group was told they would get rewarded for their own work and it did not matter if someone else in the group failed (thus reducing the hedonic relevance of others' actions). The confederate had actually been primed by the experimenter to make sure he failed the task in both groups. For the first group, the consequence was that everyone lost their money. In the other group, whether he failed or not had no significance, as all individual members got paid for their own efforts. What Jones and DeCharms did was to ask their subjects to rate how they felt about each other before and after the task was completed. The ratings they were interested in, of course, were the subjects' feelings about the confederate. For the group of subjects whose fate depended on the confederate's failure, subjects thought that the confederate was less competent, less

> dependable and generally judged in less favourable terms than he was by the group whose winnings had been unaffected by his failure. His failure was objectively the same in both cases; what was different was the relevance of his failure to the other members of the group.

How does hedonic relevance come into the model shown in Figure 1? The answer is that, although it is not a new box that can be put into the decision-making process, we can think of it as a general boosting factor: the more hedonically relevant the action is to the perceiver, the more likely s/he is to make a correspondent inference between the action and the performer's underlying dispositions. If an action is of very little relevance to an observer, s/he is less motivated to make an inference about underlying dispositions. In the example above, it was found that someone who had failed on a task was judged to be more incompetent and less dependable (two underlying dispositions) when there was higher hedonic relevance to the explainers than when there was low relevance.

1.2.1 Empirical evidence for Jones and Davis' model

Jones and Davis' article in 1965 inspired a good deal of work on people's inferences of dispositions from single observations. One of the strongest lines has been the research on how people view a statement made by another person of her/his attitudes on a particular topic.

In a typical experiment, the subject will see someone present either an expected or an unexpected argument on a controversial topic. The experiment is designed to investigate whether the degree of choice a person has in presenting an argument has any effect on the type of attributions made to account for her/his **experimental** actions, and so the level of choice experienced by a presenter is *experimentally* **manipulation** *manipulated* to test this out. This is done by telling the subject that the presenter has either been asked to give the talk by the experimenter, who specified which line s/he must take, or that the presenter chose the controversy and her/his line on it her/himself. The inference model has predictions to make about the effect of both the manipulations in the experiment. In the model's terms, whether or not the presenter chose the argument her/himself is a manipulation of the actions' non-common effects. There are more effects of making the statement in the no-choice condition than in the choice condition.

Presenter had choice	*Presenter had no choice*	
—	Not wanting to be uncooperative	*non-common effect*
—	Helping the experimenter	*non-common effect*
Expressing an opinion	Expressing an opinion	*common effect* (uninformative)

In the no-choice condition, there are all the effects of freely expressing the opinion *plus* those of going along with the experimenter: not wanting to be uncooperative, helping the experiment along and so on. So the no-choice condition has more non-common effects and, as you will recall from Figure 1 and the dinghy example, the more non-common effects an action has, the less we can be sure of its dispositional cause. So the first prediction the model makes is that subjects should be *less sure* of the presenter's attitude when they are told that s/he has had no choice in whether or not to present it.

The second prediction the model makes is about the *expectedness* of the statement. This, in the model's terms, is a manipulation of the desirability of the action's effects. To hear someone present a statement of an attitude that you would expect them to have does not tell you much about them. The desirability of, say, capital punishment is generally much higher to a right-wing politician than it is to a left-wing one, so to hear the former speak up for it is comparatively less informative. On the other hand, to hear a left-wing politician speak up for hanging will, according to the inference model, really persuade you that s/he truly believes in hanging, and is not simply going along with her/his constituents' clamour for a strong line. So, according to the theory, subjects will be more confident and extreme in their attribution of a correspondent disposition to a presenter who presents a case which one would not normally expect her/him to.

This second set of predictions has a good track record, being confirmed in a number of studies. Experiments were done in which subjects were given documents purporting to come from various people. The subjects then had to deduce from the information in front of them what the attitudes were of the people who had written the documents and how strongly the subjects felt these people believed in these attitudes. Most of this sort of experimentation was done in the USA in the late sixties and early seventies, and the documents were usually statements of opinion on such topics as the segregation of blacks and whites (Jones and Harris, 1967), the legalization of marijuana (Jones, Worchel, Goethals and Grumet, 1971), discrimination against homosexuals, busing schoolchildren and unionizing municipal employees (Jones and Berglas, 1977).

The people who were supposed to have written documents making pro and con statements about such issues were sheriffs, liberals, judges, farmers, students, homosexuals, union officials and other interested parties. The more 'out of character' the endorsement, the more the person is judged to have 'really meant it', so, paradoxically, the greater the dispositional attribution. There were other experiments on the same lines which you can read about in Box 4.

Box 4 Attributing reasons for presenting opinions

Imagine you are a subject in an experiment (as you might have been, had you been available to Jones, Worchel, Goethals and Grumet (1971)) where you are asked to read an essay someone is said to have written. It is about marijuana, and the writer wants to legalize it. You are told that s/he was given the topic, but was free to write either for or against it, as s/he wished. You deduce that s/he must be for it.

But suppose you are told that s/he was *instructed* to take the pro-marijuana line. Rationally, that means that you now have no basis at all for saying whether s/he is pro or con. You should refuse to be drawn on what you think her/his opinion is. You tell the experimenter that neither you nor anyone else has any business attributing anything at all to her/him on the basis of what s/he says; after all, it was the experimenter's wish that s/he was carrying out. However, notice that if you *did* refuse to answer the experimenter's question, you would probably be the only subject who did!

In practice, subjects in the experiment *were* willing to say something about the writer's attitude *even* when they knew that the person had written under duress. And what they said was that the writer had an attitude that was correspondent with what s/he had written: that is to say, if s/he had written in favour of marijuana, they said s/he probably had a favourable attitude towards it even though they knew that s/he had been *told* to write it that way. Foolish, possibly. But experiment after experiment found the same thing. There was always a difference between the attitudes attributed to the writers of 'pro' and 'con' essays, even when the subjects knew that the writers had had no choice. Just to be associated with the attitude, even when the subjects had been told that s/he had nothing to do with choosing it, made some of the mud stick.

Are we all liable to the same failing? Evidence suggests that we are. If you want a blunter illustration, think of advertisements which use the endorsements of well-known people. Advertisers rely on the fact that people believe that the celebrities who appear on television actually like the goods they are paid to advertise. If, like the wise subject in the Jones *et al.* experiment, you and I refused to forget the fact that the celebrities were doing it for the money and did not really care for the thing they were supposed to be endorsing, they would be out of work. But instead we often do believe that they genuinely like what they are advertising which is why the advertisers continue to use the technique.

1.2.2   Updating the model: Jones and McGillis' reformulation

information gain

The correspondent inference model was updated by Jones and McGillis in 1976 to resolve some ambiguities in its original formulation. A major plank in Jones and McGillis' platform was the notion of information gain. This is the idea that when people reach a conclusion about what dispositions a person has, part of what they are doing is *changing their previous judgements of how the person stood on that dimension.* In the earlier version of the theory, when one inferred that a person was dispositionally *generous* for example, what that meant was that one thought s/he was more generous than the average person. In the new formulation, saying someone is *generous* is both to say that s/he is more generous than the average person *and* also to say that s/he is more generous than one had thought her/him previously.

The need for this new formulation came from the fact that, in the old version, there was no acknowledgement that people could work out the desirability of the effects of someone's actions in two quite different ways: they could work out the general desirability, for most people; *or* they could estimate the *particular* desirability of the effect for this person at this time. The two might, of course, be quite different.

category-based expectancy

Going back to the dinner party example, suppose we knew that I am the couple's *boss.* Now giving an impressive meal is socially desirable, so we are less likely to assume the hostess is ostentatious. Jones and McGillis refer to these different decisions as coming from category-based ('a person entertaining friends') and target-based ('my employee entertaining me') expectancies. Category-based expectancies, at their worst, are little better than stereotypes. For example, if all one knows about someone is that she is middle-aged, very well off and lives in the Home Counties, then one may have crude, but strong expectancies about the desirability of various effects of actions she might take. We would probably feel fairly confident about making judgements about her dispositions with respect to certain actions simply on the basis of our generalized expectancies about what 'people like her' think and do.

For example, imagine if we saw her in a newsagents cancelling a subscription to the *Spectator* in favour of one for the *Socialist Worker.* Assuming that she knew what she was doing and was intending to read it (knowledge and ability criteria (Figure 1)), we would apply our correspondent inference analysis and come to the conclusion that the only important non-common effect between the two alternatives was that the latter magazine was politically on the left. Our category-based expectancy would, I presume, be that women of her apparent status would find left-wing magazines very undesirable things to take out subscriptions for; so either we can make a very confident inference about her politics, or we will sceptically cast around for entirely different explanations of her behaviour.

target-based expectancy

If we did know the person, however, that is if we have a target-based expectancy, we know something about her history, likely attitudes, personal likes and dislikes and so on. Hypothetically, these might all indicate a long history of left-wing views and activities. With this in mind, if we did exactly the same correspondent inference analysis on her behaviour in the newsagents, we would find much less information gain from the inference that she wants to read the *Socialist Worker* regularly. We might well get support for our continual astonishment that she *is* left-wing, but this would only confirm a long-held view. The *information gain* is much less than the information gain in the case where we knew nothing about the woman other than her stereotyped characteristics.

Jones and McGillis' refinement of the theory took more account of the knowledge people already had of the person whose actions they were explaining. In spite of this ref nement of the theory and its greater sensitivity to our ordinary ways of thinking, certain questions have to be asked about its usefulness as a theory of ordinary explanation.

In the next section problems with inference theory are discussed. You might like to let the descriptions of the theory and its reformulation settle in your mind first before you tackle the problems with it, so take a break at this point and return to it again later.

1.2.3   Questions to ask of the correspondent inference model

The correspondent inference model is a cornerstone of attribution theory, and yet there may be question-marks to set against it.

The first suspicion that something is wrong, that the model does not always describe real life, comes, paradoxically, from the attitude-attribution experiments which form the bedrock of evidence for the inference model's validity. These experiments seem to show that people are keenest to attribute an attitude to someone from whom it is unexpected. To the attribution theorists, this is, as we saw in Box 4, evidence for the theory. Yet one might say that the most striking thing about the experiment is that subjects never seemed to register their frank disbelief that the people presented to them would actually make the statements they were supposed to. Would people *really* believe that a general would make a public speech against defence spending, or that a Quaker would come out in favour of corporal punishment? In a sense, the consistent finding that people would attribute attitudes most confidently to people who had the least likelihood, realistically, of actually holding them was rather an embarrassment to the theory. It might well only have been the contrived nature of the experimental situation that made the subject take a 'problem-solving' approach to the scenarios being presented. If this were the case they might work out the solution to what a person's attitude might be in a very different way from the way they would in real life. In ordinary life you or I might flatly refuse to believe that a cigarette company was concerned about our health, however many sports events it sponsored. We would be wise enough to ignore the inference model and use our world knowledge about the possibility of commercial interests' capacity for dissimulation and cupidity.

Jones and McGillis are perfectly aware of this problem. Their solution to it is to propose that at some point scepticism takes over in the explainer's mind or, as they put it, that, 'as the discrepancy between expectancy and behaviour grows, the perceiver will be increasingly sceptical concerning the knowledge assumption' (Jones and McGillis, 1976, p.339). Note that the thing that the subject is thought to be likely to get suspicious about is the *knowledge* component in the actor's behaviour. Look back to Figure 1. You can see that knowledge was one of the things one had to assume before one started down the road of correspondent inference making. Jones and McGillis propose that when the person's actions are very discrepant from what one would expect her/him to do or to want, then one goes right back and questions one's assumptions that the actor really does know what s/he is doing.

This answer to the question raises the further problem of what happens when one believes that the actors *do* know exactly what they are doing. One can be absolutely certain that the cigarette company knows full well what effects sports sponsorship has. Jones and McGillis' answer seems too tame, somehow. The difficulty really is with something that lies at the absolute heart of the correspondent inference model.

What Jones and McGillis are unwilling to give up in their solution to the scepticism problem is the notion that the person is trying to make a direct (correspondent) inference from the named event (statement, in the case we are looking at just now) to the actor's underlying disposition. Not willing to give this up, they have to suppose that scepticism has its effect in some other way. What they say is that people disbelieve that actors have full knowledge of the consequences of their actions. Surely, however, it is easier and more plausible to suppose that people are sceptical not of whether the actor knows what s/he is up to, but of what her/his *aims* are, or, to put it another way, what it is s/he is trying to achieve. If so, then the theory ought to be sensitive to explainers' 're-framing', or giving a new meaning to, the person's actions. No longer is it 'sports sponsorship' but 'an advertising trick', for example. Now this is impossible using the model's formula because the whole detective system is predicated on the notion that there is a direct correspondence between the action and the disposition that causes it. Look back at Figure 1 which was taken from Jones and Davis. You will see that the task of the explainer is quite simply to 'read off' the disposition from the action: that is, the action is described as X, and the task of the explainer is to see whether or not the actor can be said to have a disposition to do X or not. There is no room in the theory for changing the name of the event which the actor may or may not have a disposition for; no room for explainers to say 'that's not encouraging sports – that's trying to sell cigarettes'.

In other words, the theory is about the sort of attributions one can make when one is constrained to believe that the action the actor is performing has one, and only one, interpretation. There is no room in the theory for different names or interpretations of the event. But since in real life every event has a good number of different interpretations, perhaps an infinity of them, there are freedoms open to the explainer that make it extremely unlikely that so constrained a model as the correspondent inference model will be able to fully describe ordinary explaining.

One might say that the model is not about ordinary explanations at all, but about problem solving. It may well be a model of how people solve the problem of what the likelihood is that person A would say or do X (where X is exhaustively described). But ordinary explanation, the critic might say, should be just as concerned with interpreting (that is, understanding the meaning of) a person's actions in the first place, as it is about going on to guessing at what caused her/him to do it.

Jones and McGillis have a reply to this criticism. What I have called a question of naming the event, Jones and McGillis would say is only really a matter of listing the effects of the action more completely and comprehensively. I call it 'an advertising trick' to advertise at sports grounds; the tobacco company calls it 'sponsorship'. But this is only a difference in the effects of the action, and the model is quite happy with many possible effects (see Figure 1). All one needs to do to accommodate what I have called different meanings is to have longer lists of effects, which, in this case, would include both 'it helps sport' and 'it advertises cigarettes'. The model can then proceed perfectly well.

Jones and McGillis would agree that it would not do to present subjects with a loaded interpretation of the event and expect them to be able to list all its effects with equal confidence, but they say that this would only mean that one has to be careful about one's choice of labels. In real life the problem is of describing the event in which one is interested, in as neutral and unprejudicial a way as possible, so as to accommodate as many 'interpretations' (effects) as possible.

You might like to consider whether this relabelling of effects is an adequate response to the criticism. Take a moment to consider two things:
(a) Is it what we ordinarily do? and
(b) What implications does it have for the sort of dispositions we can infer from behaviour?

There are two things wrong with Jones and McGillis' answer to the criticism. One is that it is an unpersuasive account of what we *ordinarily* do when we are explaining everyday things to ourselves. If it were true, then to be entirely fair and unprejudicial about the interpretation of someone's actions, we would have to go down to the bedrock of literal description of the effects of her/his actual physical movements before we could be sure we were not attributing to the action some flavour that would prejudice its interpretation one way or another. This seems at best intuitively unlikely, though of course it may, on psychological investigation, turn out to be the case. Until it does, we would be on fairly safe ground, I think, in rejecting it as a picture of ordinary mental life.

The second thing wrong with Jones and McGillis' rejoinder is that it limits the applicability of the inference model. You will recall that what the explainer learnt from using the model was that the actor had a disposition to do X, where X was the description of what the actor was doing. But if we have to describe what s/he was doing as neutrally as we can, then what sort of disposition can we attribute to her/him? In the sports sponsorship case Jones and McGillis recommend that we call the sponsorship something neutral and list all the interpretations as effects – that we list 'advertises cigarettes' and 'promotes sports' as effects – and not as names of the action. This means, however, that the only decision we can come to is that the tobacco company does or does not have a disposition to 'put up boards with its name on at cricket grounds' or 'make £20 000 available as prize money to cricket teams' or whatever it is we choose to call their action.

The more we take to heart the recommendation to describe the action neutrally, the less informative the disposition that corresponds to it becomes. But the less we describe the event neutrally, the more we are endorsing one view of the event and the less we are allowing our subjects to say that they simply do not believe that the actor really is doing whatever counter-intuitive thing we have presented her/him as doing.

On two accounts, then, the model is an unlikely description of what we ordinarily do. It is not likely that we describe actions perfectly neutrally, nor is it likely that we attribute people with dispositions to perform the actions as neutrally described. Jones and McGillis realize this: 'correspondent inference theory', they admit, 'is essentially a rational baseline model. It does not summarize phenomenal experience; it presents a logical calculus in terms of which accurate inferences *could* be drawn by an alert perceiver weighing knowledge, ability, non-common effects and prior probability' (ibid, p.404; emphasis added).

That summary of their work is very interesting. Note that they say that their attribution theory is not meant to be a description of what we think we are doing in explaining actions. On the contrary, it is a kind of formula which could describe the *unconscious* ways we silently work on the available information. The idea of developing a model about cognitive, information-processing machinery of explanations was very much in line with what was happening to social psychological theory in general at the time (in the 1970s). Social psychology was getting more and more interested in how social behaviour and social judgements are affected, and perhaps caused, by the particular ways in which the mind copes with the rush of social information.

This atmosphere of thought also helped shape the next theory which was to take Heider's observations and refine them into testable propositions. This was Harold Kelley's 'covariance model' of attributions, and the section below outlines its main principles.

1.3 Kelley's covariance model of attributions

Two years after Jones and Davis had produced their model of people making correspondent inferences about the actions of other people around them, Harold H. Kelley (1967) proposed that the observer's job was not simply to make an inference about the person on the basis of one action s/he was seen to perform, but *on the basis of whatever information was pertinent*. In Jones and Davis' original model, historical information about the observed person had played little or no part in the attributional judgement process. Kelley suggested that we ought to acknowledge that it does play a part and he specified three types of information and how they might be combined by the observer.

To describe the three types, imagine that we are trying to find the cause of this example:

> Julie had an argument with her father.

According to Kelley, we unconsciously work on three kinds of information:

(a)   Does Julie *always* fail to get on with her father? Is this something temporary or longstanding? How far does it go – does it mean she never speaks to him or just that she finds him annoying sometimes?

consistency These are questions about the consistency over time and about the modality of her feelings about him, and actions towards him.

(b)   Does she have problems *only* with her father? Has she a history of poor dealings with people generally, family or otherwise?

distinctiveness These are questions about the distinctiveness of her father as a cause of her feelings.

(c)   How do *others* in the family get on with him? Do they also find him difficult? Do people generally find that he is not easy to get on with?

consensus These are questions about whether there is a consensus about her father causing difficulties.

What one does when one puts together the answers to these three questions is to build up a case for one of three possible candidates for producing the behaviour – in this case, Julie, her father, or the circumstances. The answers could be:

(a)   Yes: Julie has never really felt very affectionate towards her father; they were not very close when she was a child.

(b)   No: she gets on well with her mother, for example, and she has no problems with her in-laws.

(c)   Yes: others do find him spiky; Julie's brothers have broken off with the family over it and even Julie's mother admits he can be difficult.

covariance model of attributions The case seems to be set fairly solidly against the father: he is the candidate who seems to account for what is happening. As Kelley puts it, the effect (of 'not getting on with') 'covaries' with (or changes alongside) this causal candidate. That is, he is the one with whom the effect seems to come and go. Julie, for example, does not have any problems with other people, so 'not getting on with' does not come and go with her. If, however, the answer to our questions had shown no pattern – say that Julie and her father never had any problems, he was well thought of, and she got on well with other people – that would leave only a rather mysterious 'occasion' to set the problem down to (rather as if there are no undesirable non-common effects in the correspondent inference model).

What we have done is to track down the candidate who is most closely associated with the event. In fact, what we have done is a bit of classic, if rather ponderous, detective-work. It does not have Sherlock Holmes' flash of brilliance, but is the sort of thing slower detectives like Lestrade, Holmes' Scotland Yard man, would work out conscientiously. Had the father been murdered, as he would have stood an excellent chance of being in a Conan Doyle story, Lestrade would have found any number of suspects on his hands, since Julie had no more reason to have killed him than anyone else (due to the *consensus* of people not getting on with him). Lestrade's methods and Kelley's covariance model work much better when the killer has a history of people dying around her/him. Take the case of the

Figure 2 Kelley's covariation detective and Jones and Davis' inference maker

famous 'Brides in the Bath' murders. Even the slow-witted Lestrade would eventually have worked out that a man whose three wives all came to a tragically early death in his bath might have something to do with the cause of their deaths. Or, as Kelley would put it, that someone who showed high consistency with the effect might be its causal source.

You will recall that when we looked at Jones and Davis' correspondent inference model, the task of the observer was to think forward, if anything, rather than back. The observer had to imagine what the expected effects of the actor's action would be and what the consequences would be of the alternatives which the actor avoided. Then the observer could infer a disposition that corresponded to the socially undesirable non-common effects, if there were any. In Kelley's covariance theory the observer has either to know, or guess at, or do some digging to find out, what the *history* of the action is for at least two of the pieces of information necessary (consistency and distinctiveness). For consensus, it is true, the observer can use contemporary information, or even simply imagine what other people would do in similar circumstances.

If we went farther, it would look as if the two models were about two different things – explanations based on guesses about the action's *consequences* (the correspondent inference model) and explanations made on the basis of guesses about the action's *antecedents* (the covariance model). But this can be put down to their different aims. As Kelley says:

> The observer's focus [in the two theories] . . . is essentially at opposite ends of the person-environment polarity. In my [model] . . . the person is concerned about the validity of an attribution regarding the environment. He applies the several criteria in an attempt to rule out person-based sources of 'error' variance. In the problems specified by Jones and Davis the observer has exactly the opposite orientation. He is seeking for person-caused variance . . . and, in doing so, he must rule out the environmental or situation-determined causes of variations in effects.

(Kelley, 1967, p.209)

In other words, the real difference between what Jones and Davis are trying to do and what Kelley is trying to do seems to be in their interpretation of what the ordinary explainer wants from her/his explanation. Jones and Davis think that the ordinary explainer wants to attribute the performer's action to some internal disposition, so their theory is about how dispositions are inferred on the basis of the choices open to the performer at the time. In Kelley's covariance model the explainer is assumed to be more open-minded about what would count as an explanation of the performer's action, and so the explainer is allowed to reach the conclusion that the action is caused by the performer's circumstances – something that the inference model saw as an impediment to an explanation, rather than a substantial explanation in its own right.

In the inference model the explainer is looking for dispositional attributions to explain actions. In the covariance model the explainer is looking for whatever candidate is consistently associated with the action – one or other of the actors, or the circumstances. Thus the covariance model suggests that the explainer rationally assesses all the possible contributory reasons for the action. However, there is evidence which suggests that explainers are less rational and balanced than Kelley believed.

1.3.1 Distinctiveness, consistency and consensus information

If people are perfectly rational users of information, then, according to the covariance model, we would use all three types of information equally well. However, McArthur (1972), early on in the experimental research, discovered that people are less influenced in making attributions by consensus information than they are by consistency or distinctiveness. This relative failure to use consensus information was seized on as a possible link between attribution theory and the work on biases in social judgement in person perception that had been going on in parallel (see Boxes 1 and 2). Some social psychologists suggested that important causes of our ordinary explanations are the *judgemental* processes we use.

Two kinds of research developed. In one, experimenters gave their subjects actions to explain, actions that they knew were likely to be perceived by the subjects as being relatively common or uncommon – and the consensus about the action was implicit. In the other, the experimenters explicitly told the subjects how many other actors had performed the action. These latter studies (which Kassin (1979) calls sample-based expectancy or explicit consensus studies) were more direct tests of consensus, since the experimenters actually manipulated the number of people that the subject was told had or had not performed the action: see Box 5.

Box 5   Consensus information

Nisbett, Borgida, Crandall and Reed (1976) in an early explicit consensus experiment presented one half of their subjects with reports of how people had acted when they took part in a psychology experiment which involved giving people electric shocks. The other group was not told about how the people had acted. Then they asked subjects in each group to read about a certain person who had taken part in the shock experiment. Subjects had to rate this fictitious participant on a number of traits and rate whether his actions were either dispositionally caused, or caused by the situation.

If people used all the information rationally and equally, then those people who had been given the information about how most subjects had acted (the consensus information) should explain the subjects' behaviour differently from those who did not have this information.

What they found was that there was no significant difference between the ratings of their two groups of subjects. Those who had been told how many other participants had done what the target had done gave no less dispositional ratings of his personality or the cause of his actions than those who had been told nothing whatever about the consensus for his actions.

In another study in the same paper, Nisbett et al. (1976) admirably tried to do something about the 'Sunday blues' that hit all of us at some time – that feeling of boredom and mild depression that can descend when there is nothing to do and the shops are shut. Nisbett et al. sent out a questionnaire to University students checking how 'down' Sunday made them feel. Then they split up their sample into three groups. One group were sent statistics telling them that feeling down on a Sunday was quite a common feeling among students. The second received the same

---

statistics plus a psychological explanation for the commonness of the feeling. The third group were sent nothing at all. Then all three groups were sent the mood questionnaires again. There was no difference in how the subjects in the three groups felt; in fact none of them were any more or less depressed at all.

These spectacular failures to use consensus information tempted some psychologists to make statements they would later regret. Nisbett and Borgida, for example, concluded from their own work that 'base rate information (such as consensus data) concerning categories in a population is ignored in estimating category membership of a sample of a population' (1975, p.935).

Some experimenters, however, had found that consensus information was not ignored. Garland, Hardy and Stephenson (1975) found that subjects ask for consensus information more than the other two kinds, in some circumstances. Wells and Harvey (1977) found that it made a difference how one presented the consensus to the subject in the experiment. At extreme levels of consensus (almost everybody does the action, or virtually no one does) then it had an effect. Kassin (1979) has done similar work presenting subjects with information about base rates one bit at a time and found, for example, that subjects tend to be over-influenced with the pieces of information that come first. Of course, the simplest explanation why subjects in the early experiments had not been much influenced by consensus information was that they did not believe it (Wells and Harvey, 1977).

The emerging picture is that consensus does have an effect if one is careful in how it is presented to subjects. The old experiments where the subject was simply told whether other people did or did not do the action as well as the performer have been superceded by experiments which do not confound the consensus information with differences in its presentation. What emerges is that consensus information does have an effect; but it is not a huge one overall, and though Nisbett and Borgida (1975) overstated the case, it is true that it is not used as rationally as it might be.

SAQ   1

Let us finish off this section on basic attribution theory with a look back at the statement from our student at the beginning of the section. If you glance back you will see that he had said many things about his neighbours. He explained their behaviour partly, at least, by attributing it to their being 'creeps'. How would the different models put forward by Jones and Davis and by Kelley account for how he came to that conclusion?

(The answer is at the end of the Unit.)

PROGRESS BOX

This section has looked at various theories of how we explain other people's behaviour.

1   Section 1.1 explored person perception — our initial assessments, or first impressions, of people:

Asch (1946) used personality trait adjectives (see Box 1).

Kelley (1950) used trait adjectives, but in a real social situation, to explore how prior expectations affect impression formation (Box 2).

Heider (1958) initiated the school of research which became the core of *attribution theory*, by noting that, as lay people, we understand others' actions as springing from something within the person or from some external pressure.

2   Two branches of attribution theory were outlined.

(a)   Correspondent inference model (1.2)
The basic assumption of this model is that you can infer an internal disposition which corresponds with (and thus explains) the other's action on the basis of choices open at the time. It thus concentrated on the *effects*, common and non-common, of the possible courses of action (Jones and Davis, 1965).

A reformulation by Jones and McGillis (1976; section 1.2.2) introduced category-based and target-based expectancies (that is, expectations of people in general and that person in particular) taking more account of prior knowledge of the person whose actions they were seeking to explain. Section 1.2.3 covered criticisms which have been made of this theory, and concluded that this model is an unpersuasive account of ordinary explaining.

(b)   Covariance model of attributions (1.3)
In this model the other person's actions are seen as being possibly caused by their internal disposition *or* their circumstances. Kelley (1967) identified three types of information which are used in attributing causes: consistency, distinctiveness and consensus. Thus prior knowledge of circumstances and of the past behaviour of the person are more important than the possible future effects of the action.

Some criticisms are presented in 1.3.1. Research by McArthur (1972) has suggested that people are less influenced in making attributions by consensus information than by consistency or distinctiveness, though this may depend on the way it is presented.

2   INFLUENCES ON ATTRIBUTION

2.1   Explaining one's own behaviour and explaining other people's: the actor-observer difference in attributions

Both the attributional models we saw in the last section were to do with how an observer explains the actions of *another* person (though Kelley's model has been extended to self-attribution). Heider had made a point about people's explanations for their *own* behaviour being different from their explanations of other people's, and Jones himself, with his colleague Richard Nisbett, has gone on to provide us with a theory of the difference.

Of course, in real life, we are all of us both actors *and* observers at the same time. We are active *participants in*, as well as being *observers of*, the social behaviour we call 'friendship', 'marriage', 'estrangement' or whatever. What implications does this have for the discussion to come?

You will have to bear in mind that to talk about 'actors' and 'observers', as I shall do, is not to say that people are one or the other, fixed and for all time. It is a shorthand. Treat the word 'actor' as if it were a label for a much longer description, which would, I am afraid, run something like this: 'the person while s/he is judging her/his own behaviour, reactions, feelings or habits'. For 'observer', you may like to read: 'the person while s/he is judging the behaviour, reactions etc. of another person'. The point to stress is that all of us are constantly doing *both* things but distinguishing between the two processes helps to identify the differences between them.

At its heart, the Jones and Nisbett theory has this central observation: 'There is a pervasive tendency for actors to attribute their actions to situational requirements, whereas observers tend to attribute the same actions to stable personal dispositions' (Jones and Nisbett, 1972, p.80) Jones and Nisbett's observation that actors tended to think of their actions as being in some way due to the circumstances they were in, while their observers were busy making correspondent dispositional inferences, had been suggested by Heider. But there is a difference between what we might intuitively think the difference between actors' and observers' explanations might be and what Jones and Nisbett are saying.

self-justification influence The difference is primarily one of the importance of what Jones and Nisbett call 'self-justification influences'. Intuition suggests to us that actors will want to blame their circumstances when things go wrong, and claim credit for themselves when things go right. Our intuition is to lay all the actor-observer differences at the door of self-justification.

This motivation to attribute causality one way or the other, Jones and Nisbett say, may affect attributions *sometimes*, but it is by no means the only, or even the most important, difference between actors and observers. For example, most things that one does and has explanations for do not involve questions of blame and credit, so it will not do to invoke 'motivational' reasons for all the differences found between actors and observers. What do cause the differences, according to Jones and Nisbett, are two factors: the *information available* to the two different people and *differences in what they do with it*.

cause data **effect data** **historical data** The first of the pair is straightforward: actors think they know *why* they are doing what they are doing (what Jones and Nisbett call cause data), what *effects* it will have (effect data) and whether they have done the same things in the *past* (historical data). The observer knows none of these things, at least not so intimately and accurately as the actor, so has to guess at them, and may even entirely fail to consider them, when it comes to explaining another's action. Thus the explanations of the two people will have different informational bases and may be expected to be different on that sole account.

Gestalt psychology of perception The second point of difference is more intriguing and less commonsensical. To understand it it is necessary to detour a little into the notions of *Gestalt* psychology. Briefly, this was an influential school of thought early on in the development of psychology. Although less so now, it has left an important mark, such as the notion that people's perception of objects in the world is not simply a matter of the objects' shape, size, colour and so on, alone: it is all these things *in relation* to other things. For example, we see the drawing in Figure 3 as a vase or as two heads facing each other according to the relation of the parts to the whole and to the salience of (the importance we attach to) the various possible outlines and what they refer to. An important aspect of Gestalt psychology is that objects are perceived as 'wholes' against a relatively stable background. In the vase/profiles drawing, the phenomenon is brought to prominence because of the two equally reasonable ways of looking at the drawing – either with the faces as the 'objects' and the black space between them as the 'ground', or alternatively the vase as the 'object' and the white as the 'ground'.

Figure 3

Experiments based on Gestalt principles refined the ideas of what would make something 'stand out' against its ground: if it moved, that made it salient; so also if it was more brightly lit; and if it changed while the other part of the image stayed constant.

What has this to do with ordinary explanations? Jones and Nisbett had naturally been as influenced by Heider's writings as had been Jones and Davis earlier. Where Jones and Davis had taken up the notion of dispositional attribution, Jones and Nisbett had taken up Heider's allusion to Gestalt notions in the perception of action. Heider had extrapolated from the perception of objects to the perception of people, and noted that when we see people behave and move about we might be applying the same sort of analysis to their actions as we might to any other part of the scene that we saw. 'It seems that behaviour in particular has such salient properties that it tends to engulf the whole field rather than be confined to its proper position as local stimulus' (Heider, 1958, p.54)

The way Jones and Nisbett put it was like this: 'We believe that important information-processing differences exist for the basic reason that different aspects of the available information are salient for actors and observers and this differential salience affects the course and outcome of the attribution process' (Jones and Nisbett, 1972, p.85). As they drily note, 'the actor's receptors are poorly located for recording the nuances of his own behaviour' (ibid, p.85): they simply cannot see themselves as well as their observer can. The observer sees a relatively stable world, with the actor moving about in it, apparently up to something; the actor sees a world whose demands are constantly changing and to which s/he must modify her/his actions and plans.

It might help to underscore the difference by imagining you have gone to see a play at a theatre-in-the-round. As you wait for the play to open, you have plenty of time to look at the scenery. The lights dim and an actress comes on, possibly in a spotlight. You see her move around the set, picking up something off a table here, rearranging something else there, going to open the door when she hears a knock. Not unnaturally, the actress is the figure against the background, and your attention (unless she is a very poor actress) will be constantly on her. You will be in the position of the Jones and Nisbett observer watching an actor whose 'behaviour engulfs the field'. If, on the other hand, you were the actress herself, quite different things would be salient for you: the props might have been improperly laid out, the lights brighter than last night, the knock at the door is a few seconds late, will the door handle stick like it did last night?, and so on. She feels the same person as last night, but the set is, or might be, worryingly different. And when the other actors come on stage the unpredictability of the scene is heightened: so-and-so may forget his lines again, the character actor might move down stage instead of up at the wrong moment, and so on. If actors with a well-rehearsed script can be so unpredictable, consider how unpredictable other people are when there is no script – in other words, in real life.

For the observer standing on the street corner or lurking at the back of the café, the situation is much the same as the play: for the actors s/he is watching, the unpredictability and the demands of the situation are much increased. No wonder that actors tend to have their attention focused on the changing world and the observers on the reacting actor. As Jones and Nisbett put it:

> These attentional differences should result in differences in causal perception. The actor should perceive his behaviour to be a response to environmental cues that trigger, guide and terminate it. But for the observer the focal, commanding stimulus is the actor's behaviour, and situational cues are to a degree ignored. This leaves the actor as the likely causal candidate, and the observer will account for the actor's responses in terms of attributed dispositions. (p.85)

ACTIVITY 2

You may like to consider if and how such a bias might have affected your observations of people which you made in the Family Observation Project. Do you feel you attributed the reasons for the people's behaviour more to them or to the environment in which you observed them? Look back at your reports to examine the influence of this bias in attribution.

2.2 Evidence for the perceptual hypothesis

Jones and Nisbett's two ideas about why actors and observers differ – the informational one and the perceptual one – have received different amounts of attention. Surprisingly, it is the latter, perceptual hypothesis which has received the lesser attention of the two; surprisingly because it is more radically psychological and counter-intuitive than the other one, and it might have been thought that this would have appealed to researchers. Let us take it first and see what sort of experiments have been done to test it out.

If attribution really does follow the line of sight and the things that are salient in it, then, Storms (1973) reasoned, if one presented people with lines of sight different from their normal ones, one should see their attributions change. In an experimental study, actors and audience were confronted with a radically different view of an event from the one they would have been used to.

Box 6   Line of sight and attributional differences

Storms arranged for two people to have a conversation and be videotaped at the same time. The angle of the cameras was important – they were pointed over the shoulder of each participant. When the tape was played back, it showed each participant either the scene as it had appeared to him, or the scene as it had appeared through the other person's eyes. Storms took measurements of how a number of people saw the conversation:

(a)   those who were not involved but simply watched it take place;

(b)   those who participated in the conversation and had not seen the videotape playback;

(c)   the participants after they had seen the videotape, either showing their own view again, or showing the view through the other person's eyes.

What Storms found was that there was indeed the actor-observer difference in the accounts given by the two participants: each said that the conversation was controlled more by the characteristics of the other person and by the situation than by their own characteristics (clearly they could not both be right). This pattern was also found for those who were shown the tape of their own point of view. However, for the group who were shown what the other person saw, their attribution about the cause of their own behaviour showed that they felt much less determined by the situation or by the characteristics of their partner. Storms' experiment was an apparently good demonstration of the Jones and Nisbett hypothesis that mere point of view could make a difference in people's account of events.

Storms' experiment looks at first sight like a good demonstration of the perceptual explanation for the actor-observer difference. But Storms himself admitted that what could have been happening was that, rather than simply getting a new sightline on the same scene (which is all that the strict perceptual explanation required), people could have also been getting *new information* which they had not had before – something which the other explanation of the actor-observer difference, the informational explanation, would have been happy with. To try and tease out these two strands from each other, Taylor and Fiske (1975) did a further experiment which kept the information constant while varying line of sight (Box 7).

Box 7   Taylor and Fiske's refinement of Storms' study

Subjects in this experiment – they were all observers – watched one or the other of two people speaking in a conversation. They were then asked to rate who had caused the conversation to flow the way it did. Taylor and Fiske found in both experiments that subjects thought whichever person they had watched had caused the conversation to go as it did, rather than the other speaker whom they had heard but not seen.

Their results supported the idea that observers' attributions of causality may be affected by what they see. However, they found that when they asked the observers to say whether the speaker's behaviour was caused by underlying dispositions (which is what Jones and Nisbett's theory predicts) they found that there was no difference between subjects' perceptions of the dispositions of the speaker they saw and the other speaker. So, although attention may affect perception of causality, it was found not to affect dispositional attribution.

This rather weak evidence for the perceptual explanation of the actor-observer difference might have been to do with the manipulation of line of sight. Taylor and her colleagues (Taylor, Fiske, Etcoff and Ruderman, 1978) tried a different manipulation (Box 8).

Box 8   The effect of context on attributions (Taylor *et al.,* 1978)

This time the experimenters arranged for the observer's attention to be caught by the fact that the target person is different from the other people to whom s/he is talking. Their subjects watched a tape-slide presentation of six people talking about various educational issues. The conversation had been carefully prepared by the experimenters to be identical for all subjects, except that one group thought that there was one male speaker and five females, another thought there were two male speakers and four females, and so on up to five males and one female speaker. (Taylor *et al.* used actors to speak the lines and spliced together different numbers of male and female voices to vary the proportions of the groups.)

What Taylor *et al.* found was that subjects saw the target person as more extreme on a number of attributes – such as her/his dominance in the group – when they were the odd one out than when they were mixed in with people of the same sex. The experimenters had taken great care that the target person did and said exactly the same things in both situations, so it was the *context* which made the difference.

We should note about these experiments that, however good the evidence is for the effect of salience of the actor on observers' attributions, it still leaves the question of the *difference* between observers and actors unanswered. It is true that focusing observers' attention on one actor rather than another has all sorts of consequences, extending beyond mere causality to observers' recall of information about the actor, whether they liked her/him or not and so on (see Taylor and Fiske (1978) for a full catalogue). There is, however, no direct and unambiguous test of the proposition that actors and observers differ because they see different things.

2.3 Evidence for the information difference hypothesis

The bulk of work on the actor-observer difference has been concerned with variations on the theme of the difference itself – what will exacerbate it, when it will appear, what corollaries it has and so on. Researchers (Ross, 1977; van der Pligt, 1981) have reviewed the difference as it appears in ratings of:

(a)   *causality;*

(b)   *inference* about what sort of person the actor is; and

(c)   *predictions* of the actor's likely future behaviour.

Experiments of all three types tend to support, at first sight, evidence that the difference does exist. Actors rate the causality of their actions as more situationally and less dispositionally caused than observers do, and they are less certain of their own future behaviour than observers are. But, even if these findings had not been challenged, surprisingly few of them actually test the *mechanisms* of the difference, as Storms had tried to do (see the discussion in section 2.2). Let us get our bearings first by looking at a representative of each of the three types of research.

(a)   Causality
The first type of research is demonstrated by Nisbett, Caputo, Legant and Maracek (1973, Study 1) who asked their subjects to say why they liked their girlfriend and also to say why their friends liked *their* girlfriends. They found that, although subjects said that their own girlfriends were pretty, likeable and so on, what they said about their friends' attraction to their girlfriends was that their friends liked 'that sort of girl'. This shows, according to the authors, that people think more dispositionally of their friends than they do of themselves.

(b)   Inference
The second type of experiment was represented in the same paper by Nisbett, Caputo, Legant and Maracek (1973, Study 2). In this type of experiment, subjects are asked to rate themselves and other people on a list of characteristics. In the Nisbett *et al.* experiment the subject had to rate himself, his best friend, an admired acquaintance and a well-known television personality on twenty trait terms, saying, for each one, whether it 'described the person well', 'didn't describe him well', or they 'couldn't say since it depended on the situation'. Results showed that people were slightly – but statistically reliably – more prone to tick the 'describes the person well' option for other people and not for themselves: they used it, on average, 14 times out of the 20 for the others, but only 12 times for themselves.

In a further study of this kind Goldberg (1978) gave his subjects a slightly different list of options: 'the word is a particularly good or accurate description of the person'; 'it is only partly, or occasionally, descriptive'; and, finally, 'the word is not a good or accurate description'. Instead of the mere twenty traits that Nisbett *et al.* asked their subjects to consider, Goldberg presented his subjects with 2800 trait words! But, fatiguing for his subjects though the task may have been, he found the same sort of results. Subjects showed a significant tendency to use the situational response for themselves rather than others, whether they were well-liked *or* disliked people. Interestingly, people the subjects felt neutral about were also seen as comparatively 'situational'. Goldberg immediately subjected his test to two replications and, impressively, found the same results both times. We shall see later, however, that there is a question-mark we can set against even his impressive efforts.

(c) Prediction

The third type of research demonstrating the actor-observer difference is that on people's predictions about the future behaviour of the person they are considering. In Nisbett *et al.* (1973) one of the studies made some subjects comply with an experimenter's request and later asked them whether they would do the same in the future. They said they would not, but other subjects who had been observing them through a two-way mirror said they would. The authors concluded that this meant once again that observers thought actors more dispositionally influenced than actors themselves did.

Taken together, all these research reports seem to add up to a weighty confirmation of the *fact* of the attributional difference between actors and observers, even if we still do not know the exact mechanism driving this difference. At this point we need to acknowledge that there are other studies that either show inconsistent results or even show that sometimes actors will attribute the cause of their behaviours to themselves and observers will attribute it to the environment.

We need to reconsider what is going on in the actor-observer difference, and we turn to the clarifying work of Monson and Snyder (1977). What they did was to bring into the discussion something that had been tacitly avoided by most people till then: the issue of who was likely to be more *accurate* in their attributions of causality.

According to Monson and Snyder, 'Actors should make more situational attributions than should observers about behavioural acts that are under situational control; by contrast, actors' perceptions of behaviour that are *[sic]* under dispositional control ought to be more dispositional than the perceptions of observers' (Monson and Snyder, 1977, p.96). That is, actors usually have more accurate perceptions of the causes of their own actions than do observers. What had not been followed up, Monson and Snyder justifiably claimed, was Jones and Nisbett's *theory* about the informational differences. Monson and Snyder updated Jones and Nisbett by pointing to likely differences in information about:

(a) contemporary determinants of the actor's behaviour; and

(b) knowledge about the history of the action – especially about whether the actor had done the action before, and what had led up to this one.

Looking at the research, what Monson and Snyder saw was that actors in the psychologists' experiments had made situational attributions for thoroughly rational reasons. Actors had generally been put in a strange situation and asked rather odd questions about unfamiliar events. If actors are more accurate than observers then it is not surprising that they should give more situational attributions of their behaviours, since their behaviour *is* to all intents and purposes under the control of the experimenter. Only when experimenters asked people in the real world about actions they had freely chosen to do and about which they knew the full history and the intention did actors make less situational attributions. This, argued Monson and Snyder, accounted for the diversity of the research findings.

It is the inconsistency of the findings that made Monson and Snyder reject not only the simple claim that the unsophisticated actor-observer difference exists, but also the claims of those who proposed a non-informational theory of why it did. The perceptual theory, for example, would have to explain why actors did sometimes attribute the cause of the event to their own dispositions. The experimental literature as a whole, Monson and Snyder pointed out, did not favour a simple theory. They recommended that we think again about actors and observers and the differences between them. We should ask ourselves this question: which of the two people is likely to be right?

Who is right and who is wrong about the explanation of someone's behaviour is of course not a straightforward matter on which to arbitrate. What Monson and Snyder pointed out was that, difficult though it might be for the psychologist to arbitrate on accuracy, at least s/he could modify experimental procedure so as to take into account differences in probable accuracy which might be accounting for the muddle and the contradictory data.

Monson and Snyder's recommendations have refreshed a hope that there may be a way of unpicking the discouraging tangle of contradictory data. With luck, new research will get through to the psychological explanation of the actor-observer difference. As this new research is still in its very early stages, we will leave it at this point and pass on to a brief consideration of another source of influence on attributions. The next section looks into the influence of those less than noble human characteristics, self-defensiveness and self-interest.

2.4 Motivational biases in attributions

Modern social psychology has sometimes been accused of looking at people as if they were just calculators – marvellously complicated ones, but calculators just the same. People say that attribution theory lavishes attention on 'cold' cognitions (i.e. calculations) and forgets about 'hot' (i.e. emotive) ones. This is not quite so. Certainly the theories we have been looking at so far – mainstream attribution models – have been about cold cognitions, but notice has also been taken of the influence of motivational biases on attribution. Heider himself made a great point of observing that passion could enter into the hardest-headed computation of cause (1958, p.172 ff), and the effects of hedonic relevance were discussed earlier (section 1.2).

Heider's observation was taken up and turned into two theories of motivational bias: defensive attribution and self-serving attribution.

defensive attribution   ### 2.4.1   Defensive attribution

Elaine Walster (1966) argued that people do not like to admit that bad things can happen to them. When they hear about an accident, they blame it on the person involved and not on the situation. By perceiving the accident in this way, they deny that bad news could happen to just anybody – so could not happen to them. Shaver (1970) took this up and made the point that if this were true, then it should be even more pronounced when the accident happened in circumstances familiar to the explainer. For example, if a road accident happened on a stretch of road on which you travelled every day, you would be more inclined to blame it on the driver than if it happened somewhere distant. The possibility of a malevolent Fate hanging over closer territory would be a powerful influence on your attribution.

Unfortunately for the theory, experiments that were done to test it were shot through with methodological problems, the most important of which was the ambiguity of the questions which the experimenters asked their subjects. Subjects were asked to say how 'responsible' the person was for the accident, and little effort was made to check how this notoriously equivocal word was understood. Ajzen and Fishbein (1977) pointed out that Heider himself had warned against being too free with the word, and had identified at least five different ways in which it could be understood. Possibly as a consequence of this confusion over the word, the experiments designed to test the theory never exactly reproduced the early findings, producing ambivalent and contradictory results. Interest in the theory dropped away as the complexities in the measurement of 'responsibility' began to be more clearly recognized.

self-serving attribution   ### 2.4.2   Self-serving attribution

This theory has had a better track record than the defensive attribution theory, probably because its central proposition is much simpler. According to the theory, people will attribute *success* in things they do to their own abilities and effort, and *failure* to the difficulty of the job and the capriciousness of chance.

This entirely commonsensical proposition has been tested in people's explanations of their successes in laboratory tasks, in teaching, in psychotherapy, and at school. The results are fairly consistent: unless it pays not to, people tend to explain success as coming from their own effort or abilities, but, like poor workers who blame their tools, they explain failure by attributing it externally. Though the pattern of results is fairly clear, some 'cold cognitivists' have argued that this could just be due to certain characteristics of the cognitive system and have nothing to do with a motivational bias. (Further details of this controversy are in Bradley (1978) if you would like to follow it up.) As a summary of the work on motivational biases on attribution it is worth saying that, though the idea is a commonsensically plausible one, the actual empirical evidence is not as conclusive as it might be.

We have now covered most of the ground of attribution theory in sufficient outline for you to be able to evaluate it as a theory of ordinary explanation – how you yourself explain the actions of your friends, relations and the people around you.

PROGRESS BOX 2

Section 2 was concerned with the difference between the attributions a person makes about another's behaviour (as *observer*) and those s/he makes about her/his own (as *actor*).

1   The central observation of Jones and Nisbett's theory (1972) is that we tend to attribute our own actions to situational requirements whereas observers tend to attribute the same actions to personal dispositions. They identified two possible reasons for this:

(a)   available information: the actor has more information than the observer – cause data, effect data and historical data;

(b)   different perception: different aspects of the available information are salient for actors and observers.

2   Section 2.2 looked at evidence for the latter, the 'perceptual hypothesis', especially Storms' (1973) line of sight and attributional differences in Box 6 and Taylor and Fiske's (1975) development of this work (Box 7).

3   Section 2.3 outlined three types of research on the information difference hypothesis: causality, inference and predictions. Monson and Snyder (1977) raised the question of the accuracy of attributions.

4   Section 2.4 outlined theories of motivational bias in attribution:

(a)   defensive attribution: people see bad events as due to the person involved rather than the situation, thereby minimizing the possibility of a similar event ever happening to them;

(b)   self-serving attribution: people attribute success to their own abilities but failure to external reasons.

(Much of the research in sections 2.3 and 2.4 is at a fairly unsophisticated stage and results have not been conclusive.)

---

3 ATTRIBUTIONS AND SOCIAL LIFE

3.1 Are explanations simply causal attributions?

In this section we look at recent criticisms of the basis of attribution theory. You will find the paper by Lalljee (1981) *essential reading* for this section, but, before you read it, we will take a look at an explanation in someone's own words to consider points of departure from attribution theory.

Below is a sample explanation from a number written by undergraduate students. The explanation which started this Unit was from the same set – look back at that again too. A number of students were asked to think of times when they had annoyed someone or had been annoyed by something a friend or acquaintance had done to them. They were asked both to describe and explain that incident in their own words.

(a) *Description* of a time when the subject had annoyed another person:

> Christmas was coming in a few days, and my room, though not a midden, was a little bit untidy. On Mum's standards, though it was a pit, and I had to clear away all my clothes and books before Christmas as far as she was concerned. This was, she said, in case a visitor looked into my bedroom.

(b) Subject's *explanation* of why his room was like that:

> I live in a 'comfortable' state in my flat, not dirty, but then again not very neat. I just like to have things all round me that I might want to use immediately or in the near future. I felt packing away and getting out again to be a drag. Usually if I take some clothes of [sic] I will just drape them over the back of the chair as opposed to hanging them up. Though I'm sure that the clothes don't suffer I end up with a pile of clothes on a chair and none in the wardrobe. I didn't feel that I should have to tidy up for some nosey parker that shouldn't be looking around other people's room anyway.

At this point you might like to examine this explanation and the earlier one for the concepts which they seem to use. Try to identify internal and external attributions in the explanations and see if other concepts are used as well.

I would be surprised if you could account for *all* that was being said in this explanation and the earlier one in terms solely of attribution of causality, or even of attribution of responsibility, though certainly these appear. The subjects seem to be doing a number of things above and beyond attribution.

Perhaps the first thing to note in this explanation is the way he describes the event before he starts explaining it. I think you will agree that the description is not neutral. We met the problem of description of events in our discussion of the limitations of the correspondent inference model (in section 1.2.3), and you can see here that any correspondent inference one could draw from the description would be almost automatically unfavourable to the actor. The description of the event seems to be, in this retrospective presentation, *part of the explanation*.

The second thing you may have noticed in the analysis of the explanation is that, even though it is clear whom the subject thinks is *not* at fault, it is not easy to find an unambiguous attribution of either causality or responsibility. The subject presumably feels that he is not to blame, and no one has a right to say that his room is a mess; but it is not clear where he is attributing responsibility, still less causality, for his room being as it is.

What is noticeable in both explanations is the subject's ordinary human concern to justify their own behaviour – either the behaviour of others as offenders or their own reaction as a sufferer. This concern may be partly served by attributions of causality and responsibility, but the subjects are using other things besides. We have seen how they use the description of the event to take them halfway there. In the explanation proper they can 'editorialize', putting in comments that do not actually explain the event but help to rationalize their claim.

One can see that in explanations like this and the earlier one the question has to be asked: what is being explained? It looks strongly as if the subjects are explaining not the *cause* of the event, but its *moral standing*. It is as if the cause was taken for granted. Explaining the moral standing of an action is a much more complex business than simply pointing to its cause, though the two may be linked. In justifications and rationalizations, a good deal of interpersonal knowledge is assumed in the explainer's statements, whereas in mere pointing to causes little or no common knowledge is asked for or given. In Kelley's covariance model, for example, the actions being explained do not have to have any significance; and the explanations need have no significance either. In fact the whole system of explanation would work just as well if we were trying to explain things in the physical world or even abstract events which did not involve other people.

In the earlier example, though, the events *are* significant and it is the attribution which is of little significance; the explainer is leaning all his weight on other things. He knows perfectly well that we will understand when he says, 'There is no explanation for what they do', that there *is* an explanation.

Much more could be said about the things that are communicated in these explanations, and it might be fruitful to wonder how much they rely for their power on certain common values being held by the listener and the explainer. Lalljee (1981) argues that attribution theory's analysis of explanations lacks this interpersonal dimension.

Set reading   (1 hour)

Now read the following paper which is reproduced in your *Offprints Booklet*:

M. Lalljee (1981) 'Attribution theory and the analysis of explanations'.

While reading this paper, take note of three important lines of argument:

(a)   whether explanations are interpersonal;

(b)   the importance of considering the context in which attributions are made;

(c)   the importance of historical and cultural differences in attributions of causality.

It is hard to disagree with what Lalljee says attribution theory lacks, but it is worth reminding ourselves what two of its strengths are.

One strength is that it gives us models of the way people select and process information to arrive at a judgement about the *cause* of social events – silent though it may be about what they subsequently do in their presentations of these causes in more elaborate accounts. The inference model and the covariance model both set out to do this. We saw that the inference model assumes a neutral description of the event being explained that is either unlikely, or impoverishes the disposition one can infer; a question-mark must therefore be set against its appearance in everyday reasoning, though it might well describe experimental subjects' problem-solving approach to social material presented as documents in a laboratory. The covariance model sets out to describe a subject's use of information in arriving at the judgement of who or what a particular event is 'to do with' and it has been useful in showing where people may fail to be perfectly rational in identifying causes. This leads on to the next 'plus' to set against attribution theory's record.

Attribution theory takes a cognitive line on social judgement, revealing information-processing mechanisms which underlie explanations. Jones and Nisbett argued that an informational and a perceptual difference could lead to the actor-observer difference that we all intuitively recognized, but which common sense would have attributed to self-justification on the actors' part. Such attempts try to set us free from the shackles of common sense psychology, with its uncritical (but not necessarily always mistaken) belief in traits.

3.2 The relevance of attribution theory to clinical and educational psychology

We do not have space in this exposition and discussion of attribution theory to do more than mention the work on *applying* attributional analyses that has been done over the last decade. Theories about how attributions affect behaviour have been put forward to try and explain problems as diverse as people's experience of loneliness, the psychological determinants of stuttering and stammering, wives' experiences of being battered and the psychological processes involved in the deliberations of parole boards (Frieze, Bar-Tal and Carroll, 1979). Theories specifically about clinical problems were put forward very early on in attribution thinking (Ross, Rodin and Zimbardo, 1969) and were assimilated by theorists with existing models of depression. It was argued that a certain pattern of identifying causes for events in one's life is associated with depression (Abramson, Seligman and Teasdale, 1978). Abramson *et al.* claim that depressed people are those who see events in their world as being beyond their control, and who believe that things are beyond their control because of long-lasting internal causes which affect many things in their lives. If this is the case, then a therapist might be able to reduce depression by persuading her/his depressed client to change her/his attributions. Changing someone's attributions may not, however, be easy, and it may be difficult to maintain the change after the end of the therapy (Peterson, 1982).

Therapy based on changing attributions does seem to have had some support for its predictions about some depressiveness attributions (Peterson and Seligman, 1980; Firth and Brewin, 1982), though it has failed to predict the depressive feelings of a sample of US college students (Hammen and Cochran, 1981) and the post-natal depression of a sample of Canadian mothers (Manly, McMahon, Bradley and Davidson, 1982). Its usefulness for therapy still has to be extensively tested, however, and it is too early to tell yet whether it will find its way into the treatment repertoire of the typical clinical psychologist.

It has also been claimed that attributions can affect children's performance at school (Weiner, 1979). If they think that their poor performance on a test, say, was due to some temporary situational cause like feeling ill on the day, then they cope better with the next test. But, if they attribute failure to long-lasting internal and unalterable dispositional causes, then they do not expect to do well in the next test and their performance drops to meet their expectations. Evidence that this is so comes from researchers who find that internalization of failure is related to such things as socio-economic status (Raviv, Bar-Tal, Raviv and Bar-Tal, 1980) and sex (Bar-Tal and Frieze, 1977; Dweck, Davidson, Nelson and Enna, 1978), with girls more likely than boys to attribute success to luck than to ability. These blanket differences between poorer and richer children and between girls and boys suggests that the attributions must be due partly to things other than accurate perception of the real causes of success and failure. The reasons for these unhelpful attributions may be cultural, but part of the reasons is the teachers' own behaviour towards the children.

Dweck *et al.* (1978) found by watching what went on in the classroom that teachers differed in their behaviour toward girls and boys. Some of these differences implied something about how the teacher wanted the children to attribute the causes of their behaviour. When a boy failed on a task, the teacher would mention lack of motivation and effort, implying that the boy *could* do better, but girls had less of this sort of explanation. Boys also attracted more criticism for their misbehaviour, but Dweck *et al.* pointed out that this only serves to make the boys more impressed by the teacher's appraisals when they came – the criticism showed that it was not due to a vague and generalized positive regard for them. The girls, by the same token, had to assume that the lack of positive feedback for their intellectual work was not simply because the teacher did not like them. After all, the teacher would praise them for other things – sitting quietly, keeping order and so on. Given then that they could not discount the teacher's lack of positive feedback as being due to a bias of the teacher's, they took it to mean that it reflected their own lack of ability.

Teachers' power to influence their pupil's explanations of their performance can be turned to good use. Dweck (1975) took a group of pupils who had a strong belief that they were powerless to improve their performance and put them through a training programme. On a series of small tasks their instructor gave them direct and unambiguous feedback about how they had done, and after a failure, explicitly referred to effort by saying, 'That means that you should have tried harder'. The programme seemed to work: not only would the pupils now mention effort spontaneously themselves in explaining succes and failure, but they would also show more persistence at tasks than they had shown before. Other experiments by Chapin and Dyck (1976) and Andrews and Debus (1978) show similar improvements following attributional retraining.

The two examples above, of depression and classroom achievement, have been the ones that have attracted the most research in applying attribution theory. Ordinary explanation is, of course, part of many more potentially improvable parts of our lives than just these two, and psychologists have recently been turning their attention to further applications of attribution theory.

Further reading

If you would like to follow up these avenues the following books contain a range of recent applications.

I. H. Frieze, D. Bar-Tal and J. S. Carroll (eds) (1979) *New Approaches to Social Problems*, San Francisco, Jossey-Bass.

C. Antaki and C. Brewin (eds) (1982) *Attributions and Psychological Change: Applications of Attributional Theories to Clinical and Educational Practice*, London, Academic Press.

---

4   OVERVIEW AND SUMMARY OF ATTRIBUTION THEORY

The last section presented you with a set of arguments critical of the assumptions of attribution theory and a set of points to redress the balance in the theory's favour. How the balance finally evens out depends on the weight given to the arguments on both sides. Each person must make up her/his own mind. Some will criticize the narrowness of attribution theory's conception of explanation, whilst some will praise the careful experimental work that has gone into testing the details of the two main models. The theory's formalization of commonsense psychology will be seen as an abrogation of the psychologist's duty by some and a positive point in its favour by others.

Review of objectives

If you glance back to the study guide you will see that we had five objectives for you in studying this Unit. You should find it a useful exercise to look back over the Unit and see if you can answer these questions. (Where the questions were addressed in detail, the relevant sections are given.)

1 What are the difficulties facing a psychology of ordinary explanation? Several problems have been raised throughout the Unit: see sections 1.2.2., 1.2.3., 1.3.1. and 3.1.

2 How has social psychology simplified explanations into manageable concepts?: section 1.1.1.

3 Describe the main attributional models and assess how the models of Jones and Davis, Kelley, and Jones and Nisbett differ from one another: sections 1.2., 1.3. and 2.1.

4 Evaluate the evidence for the actor-observer difference in attributions (sections 2.2 and 2.3) and for the existence of self-serving bias in attributions (section 2.4).

5 How has it helped explain your *own* explanations of social behaviour?: this is something you can assess from weighing up all the evidence presented in this Unit.

Further reading

For those who want to pursue aspects of ordinary explanation, the following are recommended.
(a) Person perception
M. Cook (1979) *Perceiving Others*, London, Methuen.

(b) Attribution theory
J. H. Harvey and G. Weary (1981) *Perspectives on Attributional Processes*, Dubuque, Wm. C. Brown.

(c) Ordinary explanation
C. Antaki (ed.) (1981) *The Psychology of Ordinary Explanations of Social Behaviour*, New York and London, Academic Press.

A. Lock and P. Heelas, P. (eds) (1981) *Indigenous Psychologies*, New York and London, Academic Press.

B. R. Orvis, H. H. Kelley and D. Butler (1976) 'Attributional conflict in young couples', in Harvey, J. H., Ickes, W. I. and Kidd, R. F. (eds) *New Directions in Attribution Research, Vol. 1,* Hillsdale, New Jersey, Erlbaum.

Answer to SAQ

SAQ 1

Jones and Davis would say that he had listed the effects of their noisiness and the alternatives, and had found that the non-common effect (annoying him) was generally undesirable. So he inferred a 'creepy' disposition corresponding to their 'creepy' behaviour.

Kelley would say that he had noted that his neighbours had done this before, that they had annoyed him in other ways, and (presumably) that his other neighbours were not so noisy. This consistency of the association between his annoyance and their behaviour led him inevitably to attribute the cause to his neighbours' negative characteristics ('being creepy').

References

ABRAMSON, L., SELIGMAN, M. E. P. and TEASDALE, J. (1978) 'Learned helplessness in humans: a critique and reformulation', *Journal of Abnormal Psychology,* Vol. 87, pp. 49-74.

AJZEN, I. and FISHBEIN, M. (1977) 'Attitude-behaviour relations: a theoretical analysis and a review of empirical research', *Psychological Bulletin,* Vol. 84, pp. 888-918.

ANDREWS, G. R. and DEBUS, R. L. (1978) 'Persistence and the causal perception failure: modifying cognitive attributions', *Journal of Educational Psychology,* Vol. 70, pp. 154-66.

ANTAKI, C. and BREWIN, C. (eds) (1982) *Attributions and Psychological Change: Applications of Attributional Theories to Clinical and Educational Practice,* London and New York, Academic Press.

ASCH, S. (1946) 'Forming impressions of personality', *Journal of Abnormal Psychology,* Vol. 41, pp. 258-90.

BAR-TAL, D. and FRIEZE, I. H. (1977) 'Achievement motivation for males and females as a function of attributions for success and failure', *Journal of Sex Roles,* Vol. 3, pp. 301-13.

BRADLEY, G. W. (1978) 'Self-serving biases in the attribution process: a re-examination of the fact or fiction question', *Journal of Personality and Social Psychology,* Vol. 36, pp. 56-71.

CHAPIN, M. and DYCK, D. G. (1976) 'Persistence of children's reading behaviour as a function of N length and attribution retraining', *Journal of Abnormal Psychology,* Vol. 85, pp. 511-15.

COOK, M. (1979) *Perceiving Others,* London, Methuen.

DWECK, C. S. (1975) 'The role of expectations and attributions in the alleviation of learned helplessness', *Journal of Personality and Social Psychology,* Vol. 31, pp. 674-85.

DWECK, C. S., DAVIDSON, W., NELSON, S. and ENNA, B. (1978) 'Sex differences in learned helplessness', *Developmental Psychology,* Vol. 14, pp. 268-76.

FIRTH, J. and BREWIN, C. (1982) 'Attributions and recovery from depression: a preliminary study using cross-lagged correlation analysis', *British Journal of Clinical Psychology,* Vol. 21, pp. 229-30.

FISHBEIN, M. and AJZEN, I. (1973) 'Attribution of responsibility: a theoretical note', *Journal of Experimental Social Psychology,* Vol. 9, pp. 148-53.

FRIEZE, I. H., BAR-TAL, D. and CARROLL, J. S. (eds) (1979) *New Approaches to Social Problems,* San Francisco, Jossey-Bass.

GARLAND, H., HARDY, A. and STEPHENSON, L. (1975) 'Information search as affected by attribution type and response category', *Personality and Social Psychology Bulletin,* Vol. 1, pp. 12-15.

GOLDBERG, L. R. (1978) 'The interrelationships among item characteristics in an adjective checklist: the convergence of different indices of item ambiguity', *Educational and Psychological Measurement,* Vol. 28, pp. 273-96.

HAMMEN, C. L. and COCHRAN, S. D. (1981) 'Cognitive correlates of life stress and depression in college students', *Journal of Abnormal Psychology,* Vol. 90, pp. 23-7.

HEIDER, F. (1958) *The Psychology of Interpersonal Relations,* New York, John Wiley and Sons.

HEIDER, F. and SIMMEL, M. (1944) 'An experimental study of apparent behaviour', *American Journal of Psychology,* Vol. 57, pp. 243-59.

JONES, E. E. and BERGLAS, S. (1977) 'Control of attributions about the self through self-handicapping strategies: the appeal of alcohol and the role of underachievement', *Personality and Social Psychology Bulletin*, Vol. 4, pp. 200-6.

JONES, E. E. and DAVIS, K. (1965) 'From acts to dispositions: the attribution process in person perception', in Berkowitz, L. (ed.) *Advances in Experimental Social Psychology*, Vol. 2, New York, Academic Press.

JONES, E. E. and DECHARMS, R. (1957) 'Changes in social perception as a function of the personal relevance of the behaviour', *Sociometry*, Vol. 20, pp. 75-85.

JONES, E. E. and HARRIS, V. A. (1967) 'The attribution of attitudes', *Journal of Experimental Social Psychology*, Vol. 3, pp. 1-24.

JONES, E. E. and MCGILLIS, D. (1976) 'Correspondent inference and the attribution cube: a comparative reappraisal', in Harvey, J. H., Ickes, W. J. and Kidd, R. F. (eds) *New Directions in Attribution Research*, Vol.1, Hillsdale, New Jersey, Erlbaum.

JONES, E. E. and NISBETT, R. E. (1972) 'The actor and the observer: divergent perceptions of the causes of behaviour', in Jones, E. E. *et al.*, *Attributions*, New Jersey, General Learning Press.

JONES, E. E., WORCHEL, S., GOETHALS, G. R. and GRUMET, J. F. (1971) 'Prior expectancy and behavioural extremity as determinants of attitude attributions', *Journal of Experimental Social Psychology*, Vol. 7, pp. 59-80.

KAPLAN, M. F. (1973) 'Stimulus inconsistency and response dispositions in forming judgements of other persons', *Journal of Personality and Social Psychology*, Vol. 25, pp. 58-64.

KASSIN, S. M., (1979) 'Consensus information, prediction and causal attribution: a review of the literature and issues', *Journal of Personality and Social Psychology*, Vol. 37, pp. 1966-81.

KELLEY, H. H. (1950) 'The warm-cold variable in first impressions of persons', *Journal of Personality*, Vol. 18, pp. 431–9.

KELLEY, H. H. (1967) 'Attribution theory in social psychology', in Levine, D. (ed.) *Nebraska Symposium on Motivation*, Vol. 15, Lincoln, University of Nebraska Press.

KELLEY, H. H. (1972) 'Attribution in social interaction', in Jones, E. E. *et al.* (eds) *Attribution*, New Jersey, General Learning Press.

LALLJEE, M. (1981) 'Attributions and explanations', in Antaki, C. (ed.) *The Psychology of Ordinary Explanations of Social Behaviour*, New York and London, Academic Press. (Set reading; reprinted in the *Offprints Booklet*.)

MANLY, P. C., MCMAHON, R. J., BRADLEY, C. F. and DAVIDSON, P. O. (1982) 'Depressive attributional style and depression following childbirth', *Journal of Abnormal Psychology*, Vol. 90, pp. 245-54.

MCARTHUR, L. A. (1972) 'The how and what of why: some determinants and consequences of causal attribution', *Journal of Personality and Social Psychology*, Vol. 22, pp. 171-93.

MCARTHUR, L. A. and POST, D. (1977) 'Figural emphasis and person perception', *Journal of Experimental Social Psychology*, Vol. 13, pp. 100-10

MONSON, T. C. and SNYDER, M. (1977) 'Actors, observers and the attribution process: towards a reconceptualization', *Journal of Experimental Social Psychology*, Vol. 13, pp. 89-110.

NISBETT, R. E. and BORGIDA, E. (1975) 'Attribution and the psychology of prediction', *Journal of Personality and Social Psychology*, Vol. 32, pp. 932-43.

NISBETT, R. E., BORGIDA, E., CRANDALL, R. and REED, H. (1976) 'Popular induction: information is not always informative', in Carrol, J. S. and Payne, J. W. (eds) *Cognition and Social Behaviour*, Hillsdale, New Jersey, Erlbaum.

NISBETT, R. E., CAPUTO, C., LEGANT, P. and MARACEK, J. (1973) 'Behaviour seen by the actor and the observer', *Journal of Personality and Social Psychology*, Vol. 37, pp. 154-64.

ORVIS, B. R., CUNNINGHAM J. D. and KELLEY, H. H. (1975) 'A closer examination of causal inference: the roles of distinctiveness, consensus and consistency information', *Journal of Personality and Social Psychology*, Vol. 32, pp. 605-16.

PETERSON, C. and SELIGMAN, M. E. P. (1981) 'Helplessness and attributional style in depression', *Tiddskrift for Norsk Psykologforening*, Vol. 18, pp. 3–18.

PETERSON, C. (1982) 'Learned helplessness and attributional interventions in depression', in Antaki, C. and Brewin, C. (eds) (1982).

RAVIV, A., BAR-TAL, D., RAVIV, A. and BAR-TAL, Y. (1980) 'Causal perception of success and failure by advantaged, inegrated and disadvantaged pupils', *British Journal of Educational Psychology*, Vol. 69, pp. 500-5.

ROSS, L. (1977) 'The intuitive psychologist and his shortcomings', in Berkowitz, L. (ed.) *Advances in Experimental Social Psychology*, New York, Academic Press.

ROSS, L., RODIN, J. and ZIMBARDO, P. G. (1969) 'Towards an attribution therapy', *Journal of Personality and Social Psychology*, Vol. 12, pp. 279–88.

SHAVER, K. G. (1970) Defensive attribution: effects of severity and relevance on the responsibility assigned for an accident', *Journal of Personality and Social Psychology*, Vol. 14, pp. 101-13.

STORMS, M. D. (1973) 'Videotape and the attribution process: reversing actors' and observers' point of view', *Journal of Personality and Social Psychology*, Vol. 27, pp. 165-75.

TAYLOR, S. E. and FISKE, S. T. (1975) 'Point of view and perceptions of causality, *Journal of Personality and Social Psychology*, Vol. 32, pp. 439-45.

TAYLOR, S. E., FISKE, S. T., ETCOFF, N. L. and RUDERMAN, A. J. (1978) 'Categorical and contextual bases of person memory and stereotyping', *Journal of Personality and Social Psychology*, Vol. 36, pp. 778-93.

VAN DER PLIGT, J. (1981) 'Actors' and observers' explanations: divergent perspectives or divergent evaluations?', in Antaki, C. (ed.) *The Psychology of Ordinary Explanations of Social Behaviour*, New York and London, Academic Press.

WALSTER, E. (1966) 'Assignment of responsibility for an accident', *Journal of Personality and Social Psychology*, Vol 3, pp. 73-9.

WEINER, B. (1979) 'A motivational theory for some classroom experiences', *Journal of Educational Psychology*, Vol. 71, pp. 3-25.

WELLS, G. L. and HARVEY, J. H. (1977) 'Do people use consensus information in making causal attributions?', *Journal of Personality and Social Psychology*, Vol. 35, pp. 279–93.

Acknowledgements

Grateful acknowledgement is made to Academic Press for Figure 1, from E. E. Jones and K. Davis, 'From acts to dispositions: the attribution process in person', in L. Berkowitz (ed.) *Advances in Experimental Social Psychology*, Vol. 2, 1965.

Index of concepts

POSTSCRIPT TO UNITS 8 AND 9

Points of comparison between attribution theory and personal construct theory

As you read through the first two Units of the Block, you will know doubt have picked up on several points of similarity and of difference in the approach to understanding others which these two theories take. Here we would like to draw together a few points of comparison between the theories, but this is by no means an exhaustive list: space is left in the table for you to add any others which you have noted during your reading whilst they are still in your mind. Later on, these notes will be useful to you as summaries for revision purposes.

	Personal construct theory	*Attribution theories*
Origins	Kelly was a clinical psychologist and thus the theory and methods originated in the therapeutic setting. This affects the focus of PCT (i.e. the individual and her/his view of the world) and the method used (i.e. the repertory grid, which is used interactively).	Attribution theories originated in experimental social psychology and thus aim to establish general rules about how individuals operate in a social world using (mainly) controlled experimental studies.
Philosophy	The philosophy underlying PCT is that of constructive alternativism, i.e. that we are capable of construing our experiences in as great a variety of ways as our wits will enable us to contrive.	Attribution theories are closer to a positivist view of human nature – that individuals are seeking to establish accurately the causes of other people's actions.
Methods	The repertory grid is the main method used and recent developments involve more complex computer programs to allow more detailed comparisons within and between the grids produced by different individuals.	Attribution theorists generally use experimental methods to explore the ways in which individuals attribute causes of actions and the types of attributions they make.
Focus	Essentially on the individual's view of the world in general (which sometimes includes other people).	Essentially on the relationship between people – how one person makes sense of the actions of another person.
Statement of the theory	PCT is formally laid down and was entirely devised by George Kelly. This means it has a high level of cohesion.	Attribution theories are all derived from the same basic principles, but different aspects have been explored by different researchers. There is no formal statement of the general theory.